The Author Studies HANDBOOK

Helping Students Build Powerful Connections to Literature

Laura Kotch and Leslie Zackman

SCHOLASTIC PROFESSIONAL BOOKS

New York • Toronto • London • Sydney • Auckland

Acknowledgments

Our work as staff developers took root in District 15, Brooklyn, New York, and brought us to schools throughout the New York City school system. Along the way we've been fortunate to meet and work alongside hundreds of hard-working, dedicated and talented professionals. We feel humble to think of the many people who helped us grow into the teachers we are today.

We thank the mentors in our professional lives for believing in us, guiding us, and inspiring us.

We thank our colleagues at P.S. 321 in Brooklyn, for helping to launch our journey and for continuing to be our "home away from home."

We thank the teachers, students, parents and principals in the District 2, Manhattan, schools who have welcomed us and taught us so much. The schools are: P.S. 1, P.S. 6, P.S. 11, P.S. 26, P.S. 40, P.S. 42, P.S. 111, P.S. 116, P.S. 126, P.S. 198, P.S. 217, J.H.S. 167, and The Clinton School. Their out-standing efforts are documented in the samples, generously offered, that illuminate the pages of this book.

We thank the wonderful friends we've both been blessed with who have supported us by asking about our progress, sharing their ideas, holding our hands, and encouraging us every step of the way.

We thank the families we grew up with who taught us to honor books, and continue to surround us with their love.

We thank our husbands and children, Mickey and Renny Zackman, and Paul, Micah, and Nicole Kotch, for their patience, encouragement, understanding and love, and for offering the sweetest distractions to remind us of what is real.

Finally we thank the authors and illustrators who create magic and touch so many lives.

Scholastic Inc. grants teachers permission to photocopy booklists, checklists, and reproducible letters from this book for classroom use. No other part of this publication may be reproduced in whole or in part, or stored in a retrieval system, or transmitted in any form or by any means, electronic, mechanical, photocopying, recording, or otherwise, without permission of the publisher. For information regarding permission, write to Scholastic Professional Books, 555 Broadway, New York, NY 10012-3999.

Interior design by Vincent Ceci and Frank Maiocco
Cover design by Vincent Ceci and Frank Maiocco
Cover and chapter opener photos by Andrew Levine, other photos courtesy of the authors
ISBN 0-590-49479-1
Copyright © 1995 by Leslie Zackman and Laura Kotch

Table of Contents

Our Beginnings

Several years ago, while rushing past each other in the school corridor at P.S. 321 in Brooklyn, we noticed we were each holding a copy of the same book. Immediately we paused and began talking about the book, discovering our mutual fascination with all the books by that author. We began exchanging books and sharing reactions—noticing authors we both loved as adults and as children. We discovered that Carolyn Haywood, Beverly Cleary, and Maud Hart Lovelace were important influences for us both. As children, we had read every word written by them, traded the latest books with our girlfriends, and studied the authors' pictures on the book jackets, wondering if these women really existed. We realized we'd been studying authors all of our reading lives.

In the schools we attended as children, though, there was no time or place for readers like us to formally share our discoveries. Fortunately, we had left that world behind and were now staff developers in a school with a literature-based approach to learning. In this school, students and teachers valued books and understood that making time to talk about them is essential.

Building a Community

The transformation that began many years ago at P.S. 321 energized a network of writing-process teachers who met regularly to reflect on classroom practice. Although we had often talked about our students' reading and writing, we had never thought to focus on ourselves as readers and writers. As staff developers, we decided to launch a new school year by building the school community around the books and authors in our reading lives.

As staff members discussed their favorite authors in a meeting in the library, the room filled with energy. Relationships between readers ignited as books, authors, and literary memories were shared. Bonds were forged creating a network of learners throughout the community. We realized the lifelong impact favorite authors have on readers and left the meeting determined to make a place and a time in our school community for author studies.

First we formed an after-school study group, with our first task to select several children's authors to study. With a small grant from New York City Special Educator's Support Program, we bought multiple copies of books by Cynthia Rylant, Tomie dePaola, Chris Van Allsburg, and Eloise Greenfield. We chose these authors for their wide appeal across age and grade levels. Chris Van Allsburg was the first author we studied together. Interested teach-

ers borrowed his books and copies of articles about him from the Staff Resource Center and met together to share reactions and discoveries. Lively discussions followed, centering around connections we made between the books, the author's life, and our own experiences. Lingering questions about the inspiration for Fritz (the dog who appears in all his books) led us to the school and community library, professional journals, and even a visit to the community bookstore where the author was making a guest appearance. This experience convinced us that meeting authors can inspire a lifelong dedication to reading.

We continued to study authors together and saw our community expand and grow stronger. Teachers exchanged books, engaged in informal lunchtime discussions, and began experimenting with bringing the author-study experience to their students.

As author studies were launched throughout the school, we were overwhelmed by students' responses. Classrooms and hallways were covered with books being studied; pictures and biographical facts about authors were everywhere; but what was most amazing were the conversations overheard in the lunchrooms, bathrooms, and school yard. A third grader came to school clutching her parents' latest copy of the *New Yorker* magazine, announcing to everyone in line, "Look, our William Steig made the cover!" A group of special-education students worried aloud about how Tomie dePaola would feel if they began their study of a new author. First graders clustered together talking about Vera B. (Williams) as if she were a beloved family member. Informed fifth graders argued heatedly about why Katherine Paterson chose to allow Leslie to die in *Bridge to Terabithia*. The excitement spread into the school library where the librarian was astounded by the demand of students for books by authors being studied in class. Parents reported on dinner conversations filled with talk about books and authors and on their journeys to bookstores and libraries for more books.

As we visited different classrooms immersed in author studies, the value of these investigations became clear. With author studies, all readers:

❧ **form mentor relationships with authors**. The perception of authors changes from faceless and distant names to personal and available experts offering their wisdom about the craft of writing. Both teachers and students can solve their own writing problems by reading an author's books, as well as his or her memoirs, speeches, interviews, and other biographical information. Plus, reading a selection of an author's books gives students opportunities to internalize the qualities of great writing. Students are inspired by reading the body of work and having an accessible model to emulate.

❧ **gain access to the world of authors and books.** For those students who do not see themselves as readers, these author studies, within the framework of the whole school community, provide them with a common language and a shared experience. The success of knowing and loving an author gives all students a chance to advance their journey as readers.

❧ **develop a wide range of effective reading strategies.** Participating in a community that studies a common author gives readers a variety of opportunities to develop critical-thinking strategies for creating personal meaning. Discussing responses together encourages readers' deeper understandings of process and content.

The experience of reading an author's body of work provides a context for applying high-level thinking strategies for comparing and contrasting, creating qualitative criteria, making judgments, and evaluating. And becoming familiar with various authors gives readers a sense of control and ownership and facilitates independence. Studying a favorite author gives readers lifelong strategies for selecting quality literature.

❧ **form a community of readers.** Classes engaged in author studies share a common base of experience. The author's words become the threads that weave individual responses into a cohesive and unified tapestry of readers.

Students were making powerful connections to authors. Many were determined to grow up and write in the style of their mentors. Letters to authors communicated their excitement, suggestions, and requests for advice. We were delighted to notice authors becoming heroes, influencing students' daily lives and goals.

Making changes in teaching practice is often overwhelming. Teachers need to rethink their strategies and techniques, organization and structure, and student and teacher roles. Author studies offer a framework for understanding and successfully implementing these changes. Once teachers understand the impact of authors in their own lives as readers, they are more willing and able to successfully apply this awareness as teachers of readers. We've witnessed, again and again, how students' enthusiastic responses to author studies energize and encourage teachers to continue to experiment and reflect on their role as both teachers and learners. We hope the strategies, activities, ideas, recommendations, and sample author studies included in this book help you and your students as you launch your own author studies, making powerful connections with authors as you nurture your community of readers.

Chapter 1

Author Studies:
An Overview of the Essentials

O ur professional lives have been enriched by our experiences as teachers and learners, and by the opportunities we have to share those experiences with others. We are constantly turning to the many excellent books, journals, and experts for new insights, adding fresh layers of understanding. At the heart of our philosophy—and our framework for author studies—lie our beliefs about teaching and learning:

•• Learning is best accomplished when learners are given time and responsibility to make choices about topics to investigate, books to read, learning partners, and audiences with which to share discoveries.

•• Meaningful learning is social and occurs best in a safe, print-rich environment where learners support each other in a community.

•• Learners' needs are best met by reinforcing their strengths, introducing effective strategies, and continually supporting growth through purposeful, authentic, and meaningful opportunities for practice.

•• Learners are more able to make meaningful connections between themselves and other learners, and to fully integrate content areas, when time in the school day is arranged flexibly in extended blocks of time.

•• Teachers who see themselves as reflective practitioners become powerful models and inspire lifelong learning.

The process of reflecting on and analyzing the impact of these beliefs on our daily practice shapes the work we do with children. And our evolving belief system influences practical classroom issues such as the use of time, our roles as teachers, decisions about what to teach and the most effective methods for teaching, and ways to measure learning. This chapter introduces these essential aspects of author studies to meet the needs of teachers at different stages of understanding and experience. Each is developed in more detail in upcoming chapters.

MANAGING TIME:
Mini-Lessons, Investigations, Share Meetings

MINI-LESSONS
Because we believe that learning is social, requiring extended blocks of time to practice and apply strategies in a meaningful context, we need to carefully analyze use of time.

An author study provides opportunities to focus and direct learning through short mini-lessons (approximately 10 minutes each) with small groups or the whole class. You might form a circle in the library area using mats or a rug to create a comfortable and intimate climate. To ensure order, discuss and practice routines for forming the circle at the start. Early mini-lessons may focus on such routines, as well as on strategies for active listening skills.

Mini-lessons are the seeds you plant that invite students to explore. They should therefore be tightly focused yet at the same time open-ended to ensure every student response is validated. Because readers tend to be at different literacy levels, they will explore mini-lesson topics in different ways. Their unique responses contribute to the richness and diversity of the culminating share meeting.

The books, style, and techniques of the author your class is studying are the primary source of mini-lessons. For example, if you're studying Patricia MacLachlan, you might focus on the author's strength in creating settings, the research behind those settings, connections between the author's real life and her fiction, and strategies she uses to make pictures in readers' minds. You can introduce mini-lessons through readalouds of an author's books, sharing anecdotes about the author's craft, or modeling effective reading and writing strategies.

INVESTIGATIONS

Following a mini-lesson, allow time (approximately 20-35 minutes) for students to investigate the focus issue by reading, writing, talking, and listening independently, in small groups or as a whole class. During this time, students may reread to find passages that powerfully describe settings or read the next chapter with partners and discuss their wonderings. You can confer with individual students, gathering information about their strengths, interests, and needs. This is also the time for observing and eavesdropping on group interactions. The information you gather can provide ideas for future mini-lessons. You might even invite students who are discovering new connections and making breakthroughs to lead follow-up share meetings.

SHARE MEETINGS

Whole-class share meetings (approximately 10-15 minutes each) allow time for learners to share discoveries that can be documented on chart paper as lists, webs, venn diagrams, letters, and so on. Students may share individually or a reporter for each group may summarize. As facilitator, you can make sure every voice is heard and validated, connecting ideas and learners by joining thoughts into threads of new understanding.

Share meetings can be full of surprises, often introducing unanticipated ideas that lead learners in new directions. Culminating reading–writing sessions this way completes the journey of exploration, motivates and holds each learner accountable for sharing with the community, and provides important feedback for planning future reading writing periods.

The structure we are suggesting, beginning with a brief yet focused mini-lesson, following with time for investigations, and concluding with a whole class share meeting, is effective for many reasons:

➻ First, it allows time for directed, focused whole class, small group, and individualized instruction.

➻ Second, it affords time for students to practice and apply ideas presented during the mini-lesson to their own reading and writing. This is essential, because as we know from our own lives as learners, it is the doing not the telling that allows ownership and control over new ideas.

➻ Moreover, this structure encourages students to share what they already know while learning from their peers. While students are talking together, the teacher is free to observe, confer individually with those students most in need, and assess and plan.

➻ Finally, variety in the kinds of activities (reading, writing, listening, talking), as well as in class configuration (whole group, small group, partner, or individualized learning), is built into this design.

The Teacher's Role

Because of our beliefs about teaching and learning, we see ourselves as facilitators, connecting students to books, authors, and each other. The learning community extends from the school into the home and neighborhood, as experts, authors, and parents are invited to share their knowledge. Relieved of the burden of being the only source of knowledge, we joyfully share the power and responsibility with our classroom and school community. First and foremost, we become models of active learners, sharing personal reactions, wonderings, and effective strategies during an author study. We are continually pursuing our own learning by attending conferences, reading professional materials, and networking with our colleagues. Proudly we exhibit our own process of discovery.

As teachers who spend every day listening to our students, we've learned that their interests and inquiries are our best guides in determining which authors to study and how best to connect curriculum. As we delve deeper into an author's style and technique, students make choices of personal issues to investigate. Thus content evolves, meeting each learner's personal needs and purpose, gaining momentum as the study progresses.

As you continually observe your students during an author study, you'll notice strengths and needs, question their processes, and collect evidence from their reading and writing. You can then begin to generate theories about books and authors and plan the most effective strategies for connecting them. As an author study progresses, and you reflect on what does and doesn't work and why, you can change your practice accordingly.

The Class Community

Students study authors in a variety of structures, including whole class, small groups, and individually. Groups are often short-term and flexible and can be formed by the teacher and sometimes by the students, based on both interests and needs. Cooperation is emphasized as students work together to discover as much as they can about an author in order to share their knowledge with the class community.

Studying an author and sharing books bonds every member of the class. Characters become so real they seem to live and breathe in the minds and hearts of the readers. Sharing an author's techniques and strategies in mini-lessons gives students an insider's view of the writer's craft. Communities focus around authors who become lifelong mentors.

Integrating Curriculum

Literacy thrives when students have opportunities to interact with print throughout their school day. An author study provides these opportunities. Students can read independently, in pairs, or in small groups and can listen to the author's words come alive through a read aloud. They may begin their day by rereading favorite passages or chapters (or whole picture books), spend the morning talking about the author's books with partners and the whole class, and end their day by choosing another one of the author's books to share with their families.

Choosing an author to study whose work includes nonfiction as well as historical and realistic fiction facilitates curriculum integration. While students read their books, they also gain deep understandings of math, science, and social studies concepts. They form lasting images about the past, the present, and the future, while acquiring a deeper appreciation and understanding

of other cultures. Noticing repeating patterns and cause–effect relationships and pursuing significant connections help students make meaning and understand their place in the world.

Author studies also connect the reading and writing process. As students read the words of the author, their awareness of their own readers' strategies for creating meaning is strengthened. Moreover, they notice the literary techniques and strategies of the author they are studying. As students begin their own process of writing, the focus shifts from the role of reader to the role of the writer. As they attempt to create meaning for their audience, students mimic successful techniques of the author they are studying. Thus, process and content, reading and writing, are two sides of the same coin.

Assessment and Evaluation

Author studies provide time for ongoing, practical assessment. As we listen to our students during daily mini-lessons, conferring and investigation time, and share meetings, we gather valuable information about what students are learning and how they are growing as readers and writers. Reading logs filled with lists, webs, letters, and stories are a rich source of evidence about students' growing understanding of books and authors.

Refocusing assessment on students' strengths informs our teaching and helps us form groups that foster risk-taking, support, and success for every member of the community. Teachers, students, and parents can then reflect on the learning process, make plans for future challenges, and actively participate in evaluation. This kind of assessment enhances understanding of the reading and writing process and enables a stimulating and nurturing literacy environment.

Chapter

2

Choosing an Author

Finding the right author to fit your particular situation is your first and most important decision. We recognize how overwhelming this task may seem to teachers just setting out to discover the world of children's literature. Many teachers begin by visiting the local bookstore or library, choosing one author to study and reading all of his or her books. It's comforting to keep in mind that your list of familiar authors will grow as you share with your colleagues and enlist the help of your students in discovering new authors. Getting to know the work of even one wonderful author will allow you to begin to address the needs and interests of your students through an author study. In fact, one favorite author can probably help you teach everything your students need to learn!

We've outlined some influencing factors and made some recommendations to help determine your choice of author to study. Then it's up to you to fill in the gaps with your own discoveries and favorites.

Students' Interests

Getting to know your students is essential so that your teaching is informed and shaped by their interests and needs. There are so many authentic opportunities throughout the day for gathering this valuable information.

During conferences, book talks, and share times, listen and look for clues about topics and authors to study. Written responses to books and students' notebooks are also wonderful sources. Surveys are another way to tap into reading and writing behaviors and preferences. We once heard a group of second graders talking about insect bites while lining up for dismissal, connected this to their fascination during an earlier read aloud of a book with a unique design format, and thought of Eric Carle for a possible author study. Other areas of interest and possible authors to study follow:

Interests	Author Study Suggestions
Buildings and Architecture	David Macaulay
Earth and Space	Seymour Simon
Transportation	Donald Crews
Dinosaurs	Aliki
Animals	Leo Lionni
Sibling Relations	Judith Viorst
Native Americans	Paul Goble
History	Milton Meltzer
Medieval Times	Elizabeth Winthrop

Students' Reading Needs

The same opportunities for discovering more about your students' interests will also provide valuable information about their needs. Consider students' reading abilities when choosing and organizing an author study. (Sample author studies in Chapters 6 and 7 explore reading needs, organization, and grouping in more detail.)

There are times when you might choose an author whose work is above the independent levels of your students. Reading aloud is one way to share these books, regardless of students' abilities or needs. For students who are frustrated by not being able to read books that are popular with their age group, reading aloud not only gives them access to the text, but also inspires them to attempt independent rereadings with familiarity and built-in support. These students need many successful literacy experiences to develop their self-confidence as readers and need opportunities to study authors they can read independently, as well. Descriptions of three broad reading stages with author suggestions for independent reading follow:

Reading Needs	Characteristics	Author Study Suggestions
Early Emergent Reader	• beginning to develop strategies for word attack • developing sight vocabulary • expects print to make sense • relies on illustrations	Frank Asch Rita Golden Gelman Bill Martin, Jr. Dr. Seuss Rosemary Wells
Later Emergent Readers	• growing confidence • larger repertoire of strategies • growing sight vocabulary • begins to self-correct	Marc Brown Miriam Cohen Syd Hoff Leonard Kessler Arnold Lobel Cynthia Rylant Gene Zion Harriet Ziefert
Transitional Reader	• capable of more silent and independent reading for longer periods of time	David Adler Ann Cameron Matt Christopher Judy Delton

Reading Needs	Characteristics	Author Study Suggestions
	• still needs support for strategies and choices • begins to explore genre	Patricia Reilly Giff Else Holmelund Minarik John Peterson Barbara Ann Porte Marjorie Sharmat
Fluent Reader	• explores wider variety of reading materials • approaches text with confidence, concentration, and independence • adjusts reading style to content • reflects on process and content	Betsy Byars Paula Danziger S. E. Hinton E. L. Koningsburg Gordon Korman Lois Lowry Katherine Paterson Barbara Park Louis Sachar Robert Kimmel Smith Jerry Spinelli

Students' Writing Needs

Sometimes we choose an author to help our students to become better writers. Our experience shows that the most effective writing teacher is an author whose books demonstrate successful literary techniques. Examine students' writing to learn more about their strengths as well as their needs. Let this information guide you in selecting authors who can serve as mentors to your students. Remember that no matter how old students are, picture books are strong writing models. The following list links common writing needs with both picture book authors (p) and novelists.

ONE AUTHOR FOR EVERYONE

If you're working with heterogeneous grouping, you might look for authors who have published books at various levels of reading abilities. Here are some who fit the bill:

Lucille Clifton
Roald Dahl
Patricia Reilly Giff
Eloise Greenfield
Johanna Hurwitz
Patricia MacLachlan
Katherine Paterson
Gary Paulsen
Cynthia Rylant

Writing Needs	Author Study Suggestions
Story Plot	Ezra Jack Keats (p) Judy Blume
Developing Characters	Anthony Browne (p) Katherine Paterson
Setting	Patricia MacLachlan (p) E. B. White
Details	Barbara Cooney (p) Cynthia Rylant
Poetic Language	Jane Yolen (p) Roald Dahl
Vocabulary	William Steig (p) Paula Fox
Surprise Endings	Chris Van Allsburg (p) Robert Cormier

Assessing Reading and Writing Needs

We've found the following techniques most helpful in assessing and evaluating the reading-writing needs of our students as we consider possible author studies. We like to use them over the course of the school year, in the beginning, middle, and at the end.

READING-WRITING ATTITUDE SURVEYS

In order to understand how best to teach our students each day and before we can move them ahead as literate people, we need to know their histories. Early experiences with reading and writing certainly influence feelings about reading, interests and concerns, self-esteem, attitude, and willingness to take risks.

An excellent way to explore this rich source of information is through attitude surveys, such as the one Nancie Atwell included in *In the Middle*. You can use the questions to plan mini-lessons, to collect data about shared interests, for peer interviews, as sources for webs and lists, and to publish and

share individual time lines and oral histories. Shared stories of readers' lives—about favorite books, genres, authors, and their mentors and break-throughs—all help you to know your students and bond them together into a community of readers and writers.

Parents are another excellent source of information and often enjoy the opportunity to participate in surveys. You might write a letter to parents at the beginning of the school year, asking them to share their child's favorite leisure activity, book, author, reading memory, or home reading ritual.

ANECDOTAL OBSERVATION (KID-WATCHING)

Close observation during reading and writing time yields important information about the way students interact with print, including attitudes of students, learning styles, social behavior, interests, strengths, and needs. You can begin this kid-watching by simply putting books of different genres and levels in front of students. Observe how students hold the books, their focus of interest and attention span, and comments and conversation.

This eavesdropping allows you to "listen" intently to the thinking processes of your students, helps focus inquiry, and leads to conferences with students that inform teaching. Teachers often share their observations with students: "I've noticed you put that book down before you finished reading it and I'm wondering why." Students' responses to questions like this provide rich data for understanding strategies, needs, interests, and literacy levels. At the same time, an honest dialogue between readers is launched, allowing teachers to share their own successful strategies as readers.

Many teachers carry a notebook around with them as they observe, con-fer, and share with students. These anecdotal records help in reflecting on observations, planning mini-lessons, and making group decisions and provide teachers, students, and parents with concrete evidence of literacy acquisition.

CHECKLISTS

Many excellent checklists are available for all literacy levels, listing essential strategies and behaviors to help teachers know what to look for as they get to know their students. You may want to use the samples in Appendix D (page 150) as reference to create your own checklist. When using a checklist, it is important to keep in mind that children develop in their own unique ways and at their own rates. Checklists are meant to provide a framework for understanding the kinds of behaviors you want students to develop as they are immersed in a positive, nurturing, print-rich environment.

One of the best ways to understand the strategies students use successfully as readers and writers is to sit beside them as they engage in these tasks. Watch and listen for individual strengths and needs in creating meaning around print. Point out all the things students are doing effectively as readers and writers. You might connect students to models, perhaps other students, themselves, or authors, for example, "You used the same strategy as Cynthia Rylant when you focused on the everyday details from your life in your story." This important feedback allows students to become aware of successes, thus incorporating them into their repertoire of effective strategies.

Students' Backgrounds

How often have you seen knowing looks of recognition on readers' faces when they "see themselves" in books? We try to ensure that all of our young readers and writers have that experience by carefully selecting authors. Students' ethnic, gender, racial, and cultural backgrounds are all important factors to consider. Reading books that offer a range of perspectives also serves to heighten awareness that leads to appreciation and understanding of other cultures. Some authors whose work helps us see our differences, as well as our common humanity, include:

Ann Grifalconi	Allen Say
Rachel Isadora	Gary Soto
Patricia McKissick	Yoshiko Uchida
Nicholosa Mohr	Laurence Yep
Walter Dean Myer	Ed Young

Teachers' Interests

As whole-language teachers, we have seen the power of becoming literacy models for our students and certainly want to share our own enthusiasm and interest for particular authors with them, possibly as author studies. Teachers who share their interests, as well as their strategies for pursuing knowledge, offer students a path for exploring their own passions and interests. One of our colleagues shared her childhood love of Margaret Wise Brown's books with her first-grade class, inspiring a class author study. As the classroom filled up with books and enthusiasm, parents stopped by to thank the teacher for allowing them to relive their own childhoods with their children and this author.

Exploring New Genres

Our experience has taught us that readers tend to develop strong genre preferences over time. Exposing students to a variety of reading experiences allows them to challenge themselves and become more informed about their choices. We've listed some prolific authors who express themselves in a variety of genres, as well as authors who are genre specialists.

Genre	Author Study Suggestions
Biography	Russell Freedman Jean Fritz Mike Venezia
Fairytales	Jan Brett James Marshall Jon Sciezka
Fantasy	Susan Cooper C. S. Lewis Maurice Sendak
Folktales	Verna Aardema Ashley Bryan Jane Yolen
Historical Fiction	Collier and Collier Scott O'Dell Elizabeth George Speare
Memoir	Tomie dePaola Mem Fox Patricia Polacco
Mystery	John Bellairs Ruth Chew James Howe
Photo Essay	Isaac Asimov Bruce McMillan Patricia Lauber

Genre	Author Study Suggestions
Picture Books	Eve Bunting Arthur Yorinks Charlotte Zolotow
Poetry	Paul Janeczko Nancy Larrick David McCord
Science Fiction	Lloyd Alexander Bruce Coville Madeline L'Engle
Short Stories	Nicholosa Mohr Cynthia Rylant Gary Paulsen
Wordless Picture Books	Raymond Briggs Mercer Mayer David Weisner

AUTHORS WHO WRITE IN A VARIETY OF GENRES

	Poetry	Memoir	Fantasy	Picture Books	Folktales	Novels
Eve Bunting	✗			✗		✗
Lucille Clifton	✗	✗		✗		✗
Roald Dahl	✗	✗	✗	✗	✗	
Tomie dePaola		✗		✗	✗	
Eloise Greenfield	✗	✗		✗		✗
Patricia MacLachlan	✗		✗		✗	
Katherine Paterson		✗		✗	✗	✗
Cynthia Rylant	✗	✗		✗	✗	✗
Marilyn Singer	✗		✗	✗		✗

Availability of Books

You might already have amassed a wonderful collection of books by an author. Or perhaps your school has a generous supply of books available to your class. This alone might lead you to an author study. The number of books will help determine the organization of the study. You may have single copies of several picture books, which would make for a good read aloud study. If you have a few copies of four different books by one author you might consider forming small groups. If there's an author you would really be interested in studying, but you simply don't have the books, add that author's name to your wish list and start building up a collection. (For more on gathering books together for a study, see page 28.)

Integrating Curriculum

We can't imagine teaching fourth graders about the American Revolution without Jean Fritz by our side. There are many authors who have passions about certain topics that will support your curriculum needs (see Integrating Curriculum, Chapter 9).

Author's Message

At times you may choose an author whose message is one your students need in their lives. Often, authors' messages endure long after the studies, influencing attitudes and behavior, strengthening and unifying classroom communities. Many authors weave powerful messages into their words and illustrations. Here are some suggestions:

Message	Author Study Suggestions
Value of Family	Eloise Greenfield Nicholosa Mohr Vera B. Williams
Struggle for Survival	Helen Cowcher Jean Craighead George Gary Paulsen
Spirit of Discovery	Anno Joanna Cole James Cross Giblins

Message	Author Study Suggestions
Wisdom of Grandparents	Tomie dePaola Virginia Hamilton Patricia Polacco
Miracle of Transformation	Anthony Browne Roald Dahl William Steig
Power of Friendship	Janet and Allan Ahlberg Beverly Cleary Arnold Lobel
Joy of Laughter	James Marshall Louis Sachar Arthur Yorinks
Need to Create Beauty	Bryd Baylor Barbara Cooney Thomas Locker

Contact with Authors

Sometimes opportunities to meet authors come your way—through professional conferences, bookstore readings, and so on. Once in a while, this leads to the chance to invite an author into your classroom, enabling everyone to get first-hand insight into an author's work. One of our students wrote to Robert Kimmel Smith telling him how much his books were enjoyed and inviting him to visit the class. His surprise acceptance launched a schoolwide author study! (For more on arranging author visits, see Chapter 11.)

Chapter

3

Creating a Language-rich Environment

After you've chosen an author to study, it's time to consider how you'll create a literate environment that will foster connections between your students and the study you are about to begin. Language-rich environments provide open invitations for students to endlessly explore opportunities to become readers and writers. The value of language is powerfully demonstrated through an environment saturated with meaningful print, including all kinds of books, magazines, student writing, quotes, newspapers, lists, class charts, author information, letters, and more. A classroom library filled with a variety of wonderful books and comfortable settings beckons students to read, listen, talk, and write together.

Teachers and students can create this environment together by gathering resources, creating an author study center, preparing a special place for writing, and extending the environment into the home and school community. More on each of these follows.

Gathering Resources

COLLECTING BOOKS

As soon as you choose an author but before launching your study, we suggest that you begin to gather books. Knowing the number of books available will help you decide whether to present your study through read alouds, by students reading their own books, or a combination of the two. Possible sources of books include:

Your own classroom library. If you take a good look through the shelves in your classroom library, you might be surprised to find you already have a collection of several books by the same author. Involving students in the search for books gives them opportunities to reexamine and reorganize the class collection, too. Many classes we know have launched an investigation to research the best ways to display their classroom library collections. Trips to school, public, and classroom libraries can suggest possible strategies for organizing and displaying books. Some of the most appealing libraries we've seen have included author baskets, where books by a particular author are displayed along with supporting materials.

Your school library. Most school librarians would be delighted to put together collections of books for author studies.

Several librarians we know even use these requests to guide book orders and build author collections.

Personal book collections. Invite students to check their own book collections at home and to visit local libraries to check out their shelves. This is an opportunity to get parents involved as well. Ask colleagues if they might have some books to lend your class for your author study. It's an opportunity to share what your class is doing. You just might start some interesting discussions—and build professional ties, too. Some schools have launched schoolwide author studies as a result of two teachers getting things going in their own classrooms and sharing with each other.

School book-club orders. One of the easiest and least expensive ways to build up your classroom library and author study collection is to purchase books through the book-club orders your students use. You can exchange bonus points that you accumulate for books. Many book clubs feature books by one author, along with information packets, each month. The prices are reasonable, and you can purchase books for your professional and personal collections through the clubs as well.

Book fairs. Many schools sponsor book fairs throughout the school year. This is an opportunity to purchase books and support schoolwide fund-raising efforts at the same time.

Bookstore trips. A visit to a local book store provides an opportunity to purchase books, as well as investigate how experts lovingly display them. We know schools where groups of teachers arrange for special visits to preview new books and talk with shop owners (and return laden with books they couldn't resist buying to share with their students!). With advance notice, most bookstore owners are eager to accommodate class trips, too. Hopefully, bookstore visits will become a lifelong ritual for all readers.

Flea markets, stoop sales, garage sales. We never pass by one of these sales without checking out the children's books. We've come across some wonderful books to add to our libraries for as little as a quarter.

COLLECTING AUTHOR INFORMATION

Making connections between an author's work and his or her life is an integral part of an author study. Joyful readers know the delight of hearing favorite authors being interviewed on television or reading about them in newspaper articles. Through experiences like these, readers are able to get "inside information" that leads to insight of the author's craft. (For more on sharing author information, see page 40.)

It is important to start collecting information as it comes your way. We urge you to keep files to stay organized, so that when you do decide upon an author to study, you might already have some information handy for your author basket or author study center. In some schools we know, teachers maintain a file system that is accessible to all, in the school libraries and staff resource centers. Other sources of author information include:

Book jackets. A picture of the author, accompanied by a short biographical sketch, is often included on a book jacket. It's not always enough to satisfy curious readers, but it's a taste.

Book-club newsletters. The magazines that enclose the book-club order slips for students are filled with wonderful information and ideas about books, genres, and authors, including interviews with and letters from featured authors. We always clip and add these special pages to our files. Book clubs sometimes offer special author packets that include tapes. Some are even venturing into video interviews. These materials may be available for bonus points or included in orders of certain amounts.

Professional journals. There are several journals that we highly recommend you subscribe to. (For a complete list, see page 144.) These journals are filled with articles about whole language issues and concerns and often review the latest children's books. Fascinating articles written by and about children's authors, illustrators, and other members of the writing profession give us a better understanding of the writer's world. We always add copies of these articles to our author files.

Publishers and bookstores. Most publishers are delighted to send out whatever they can to support your author study and even help you set up author visits. We have received beautiful posters, bookmarks, author biographies, glossy photographs, book jackets, and even sample books from publishers. Check with the children's book publicity departments to see who handles these requests. Bookstores often hand out promotional packets when new books are published, especially when an author is scheduled to appear for a reading and signing session. For publishers' toll-free numbers, call the 800 directory, (800)555-1212, also a no-charge call.)

Special books about authors. It's no coincidence that as more and more children learn through an integrated process approach, the need arises for books that also give insight into the craft of writing. It is so wonderful to see that there are more and more books available these days that are specifically about children's book authors. Collections such as *Meet The Authors and*

Illustrators by Deborah Kovaks and James Preller (Scholastic Professional Books) provide background information, inspirational quotes, and tips from well-loved authors and illustrators. In addition, many popular children's book authors and illustrators are publishing memoirs and autobiographies that enhance studies of their work. Start collecting these resources! (For suggested titles, see pages 130–131.)

Author presentations. If you have an opportunity to hear a favorite author speak, don't pass it up. We've had many chances to meet authors at conferences or at bookstore readings and signings and have rarely been disappointed. We bring back pages of notes and delightful anecdotes to share with students and colleagues, connecting authors to books in a powerful way.

Creating an Author Study Center

Finding a special place to display books, biographical information, as well as charts that document discoveries, will encourage and facilitate students' connections to the author. Invite students to help you decide where the best place for this center may be.

A bulletin board featuring the author's picture and biographical information, a clothesline to hang the charts your class will generate, a table with a cloth to beautifully display the author's books, a bookshelf to hold student writing inspired by the author study are all possible ways to demonstrate the important place the author study commands in your classroom. Display students' posters advertising upcoming or ongoing studies outside your classroom to extend the environment and inspire schoolwide interest and enthusiasm.

Creating a Place in the Writing Lives of Our Students

Just as we provide a special place in our classroom for our author study, we also provide a special place in our students' writing lives for the study, enabling them to record ideas, think about research issues, reflect on wonderings and connections, and experiment with the author's style and techniques.

Although class charts will document shared discussions, we also suggest that students, or groups, maintain their own notebooks. There are many ways

to design author study notebooks. A few suggestions follow:

→ Set aside a special section in the general reading response notebooks.

→ Create special individual folders, personalized by students, for each author study. Simply fold large sheets of construction paper in half, or provide blank manila file folders. Students can use paper fasteners to add notebook paper, adding or removing pages as the study grows.

→ Have students purchase a few composition notebooks at the beginning of the school year. One becomes a reading response notebook for independent and group reading, another becomes a writing notebook, and a third is reserved for author studies. As each new author study is launched, students can fold down a page and label it with the author's name, easily creating separate sections.

→ If you organize response groups during an author study you might use a single folder or notebook for each group, with each student taking a turn as the response entry recorder.

In some classrooms, students keep their notebooks in their desks, while others, organized by groups, create storage baskets to store both notebooks and books. Since there are many options, we suggest you choose the management system that works best for you.

Extending the Environment

One of the most effective ways of enhancing a literary experience is to share it with other readers. In fact, research on peer learning supports the positive value of shared learning for all participants. Author studies provide endless opportunities for shared learning not only within your classroom, but also throughout the school community. Three approaches to extending your learning environment follow.

Table of Contents

Page(s)	Activity(ies)
1.	Photo of Author
2.	Facts of Author
3.	Books I Read
4.	What I Know / Want to Know
5.	Wonderings / Clues
6.	Summary / Chapter 1
7.	Questions / Answers
8.	Words I Learn
9.	Character Activities
10.	"11" Analysis
11.	Web - Characters Activities
12.	Letter / Diary / Illustration
13.	Chunks
14.	Conversation
15.	Web - Lucas' Problem
16.	Time Line
17.	Predict The Future
18.	Chart
19.	Author Style Web
20.	Author Style Story
21.	Letter
22.	

INTERCLASS READING BUDDIES

The same considerations we urge teachers to think about when forming classroom partners and groups should be given towards forming interclass reading buddies. Teachers might meet first to discuss matches, with the understanding that changes may have to be made. We recommend keeping partners together for the duration of the collaboration, if possible.

One fifth-grade teacher paired up with a first-grade teacher to form reading buddies between the two classes but encouraged the pairs to meet in groups of four. This way, if a student was absent during an interclass visit, the partner would still be part of a group. Think about the best way to physically accommodate and manage two classes divided up into many pairs. You may want to move to a bigger space, or consider using hallways as additional space. Classes could meet as often as scheduling permits, but we do suggest that the time allotted for the meeting be sufficient to allow for traveling to and fro, leaving enough time in between for students to really get to work together. Plan on at least 45 minutes per session.

Prepare students in both classes for the experience by discussing behavior expectations, active listening skills, interpersonal amenities, and author study activities. It's also a good idea to spend some time in each class, and perhaps together, on getting and giving feedback on how things are working out between partners. You might present mini-lessons at the beginning of a visit to set a focus. Or, students could decide on their own how to spend their time together. It's possible that some buddies will read, some may choose to write an original piece, and others might want to talk about and respond in writing to the books they are sharing. Reading buddies can maintain collaborative response notebooks that can be as simple as filling in date, title, pages read, and signatures of both partners. For more elaborate entries, students can include webs, story maps, and so on. (For more information and ideas on responses, see Chapters 4 and 5.)

SHARING A STUDY

You might consider sharing your author study with another class on the same grade level by inviting the class in to see your display, sit in on read alouds, join in response discussions, and help you celebrate a successful study. Some classes we've worked with design and send invitations to other classes on their grade to attend a student reading of work by the author being studied. Strategies for effective read alouds can be modeled during mini-lessons by both teachers and students. Build fluency and ensure a powerful read aloud by allowing time in class for students to select and practice reading excerpts. You could also begin by having students write letters to peers

telling about their author study. Two classes could even collaborate and form groups across class lines to study the same author or compare discoveries about two different authors.

READING AND WRITING TOGETHER

Students of varied ages enjoy reading to each other, talking about the books, and sharing their writing. It's especially helpful when one of the classes, older or younger, has had some previous author study experiences to share. A sixth-grade Chinese bilingual class studying work by Anthony Browne was captivated by his illustrations and very accessible text. These students were inspired to write their own versions of *Things I Like*. Their teacher arranged for them to meet with a second-grade Chinese bilingual class in the school so that they would have another audience for their writing. The meeting was a success and the classes decided to collaboratively study Eric Carle, a new author for both classes. As students continued to meet, they shared their original writing inspired by Carle's work.

Partnerships like these benefit both students and teachers. Working collaboratively encourages teachers to pool resources such as books and biographical information. In addition, sharing responsibilities allows teachers to observe student interactions and reflect together on their practice. Students benefit by serving as mentors for each other and forming strong connections around books. Entire schools have become caught up in author study excitement that began with a collaboration between two classes.

HOME–SCHOOL CONNECTIONS

Children who are immersed in an exciting author study are often eager to share their discoveries with their families. Their enthusiasm delights and inspires many parents to become involved, strengthening ties between home and school. Because we know parents are an essential resource but, like us, are busy people with varied demands on their time, we offer several ways for them to support a classroom author study. Here are some ideas.

Letters to parents. A letter to parents about an author study builds enthusiasm and excitement and invites parent participation. Some teachers send the letter before the author study begins, while others wait until the study is underway. In either case, the letter gives parents insight into the author study process and encourages their participation. This authentic opportunity for letter-writing allows students to participate in making decisions about what to say and how best to say it. You might send one class-composed letter or individual ones, asking parents to contribute books or a small donation to help purchase books, volunteer time to join author study activities, or help in follow-up homework assignments. This dialogue may continue throughout the author study and culminate with an invitation to join the author study celebration (See Appendix G.)

Book in a bag. Research shows that children who read at home are likely to become lifelong readers; therefore, homework that helps parents create a daily reading ritual is essential. A ritual many teachers build into author studies is for children to take home a book each night to share and enjoy with their family. Rereading favorite books at home with a family member builds on familiarity and leads to competency and fluency. Depending on books available, you might want to make this a daily or weekly routine. Students can place borrowed books in special bags to ensure their safety and emphasize the importance of the activity. You may want to use large recloseable bags and ask students to design their own name labels. To extend the Book in a Bag concept, you might try these ideas:

➡ Ask students to take their response journals home with the book in a bag. Children can make additional entries at home that record their reactions, wonderings, and connections. Parents and siblings can participate by entering their own reactions in the journal and keeping an ongoing record of shared titles. Children enjoy seeing family members as readers and writers, and the journal becomes a valuable record of family reading time. You can contribute to the dialogue by responding to students and their families with your own entries in the journal. Many teachers begin their day by sharing responses to the Book in a Bag and end their day with children selecting the next book to take home that night. Thus, the day begins and ends with readers talking about books shared with family, a vital part of the community (See Appendices H and I.)

➡ Another ritual that encourages family literacy is inviting families to write letters about their shared reading experiences. You might place an envelope in the back of each book in an author study collection. When children take books home, they can read what other families think about the books and authors and then record their own thoughts. Bind these letters into a book to document the connection between home and school. The book then becomes part of the literate environment (See Appendix J.)

Read-aloud visits. Parents can participate in author studies by volunteering to come to school and read to the class. Students enjoy hearing stories read by different voices, and parents enjoy sharing their love of reading with their children. These visits offer you more opportunities to sit back and observe students with other adults and reflect on what they see and hear. Classrooms are enriched by visits from joyfully literate adults who serve as

role models. Likewise, parents are enriched and impressed by their children's natural exuberance, enthusiasm, and honest responses.

Parent workshops. Another strategy for strengthening bonds between home and school is to offer a series of parent workshops, held at convenient times to accommodate parents' schedules, led by teachers involved in author studies. Many parents will welcome the opportunity to read and talk about books in social groups. Teachers leading these workshops can use the same books that students are studying, as well as the same strategies for connecting these books to readers. The whole group may study one author with smaller groups forming around particular titles. Or parents may form small groups from a menu of book choices.

When parent readers participate in author studies, they become aware of the excitement and power of shared reading. They can't help but bring that energy back home to their families. Moreover, when teachers have the opportunity to lead parent workshops, they have natural reasons for collaborating with other teachers and parents. They find that the experience of leading these workshops forces them to reflect on what they know and believe about teaching and learning, to sharpen and refine their skills, and to reenergize their commitment to their craft. Teachers become empowered when they serve as leaders, in turn empowering parents through their interactions with other adults around shared books.

Chapter

4

Connecting Students with Authors

There are many ways to encourage student response and develop connections to an author's work that we successfully use in a variety of classroom structures. From lists of books to choral readings and character parties, these activities can provide the focus for mini-lessons that inspire further investigation by students as a whole class, in small groups, or independently. You can explore these activities with your students in any sequence that fits your class structure, builds interest, satisfies curiosity, and brings delight, for there is no one right way to launch an author study.

We've included lots of samples of classroom charts documenting student discoveries that began during mini-lessons, grew during reading investigations, and concluded with discussions during share meetings. These charts can become part of the author center in your classroom. As the study progresses and students read more books, you can refer back to these charts to add to and confirm connections to the books and the author. This is also an opportunity to model strategies for spelling, neatness, and accurate writing. When possible, turn this responsibility over to students by asking them to respond in their own notebooks or to serve as recorders for group and whole-class charts.

LIST OF BOOKS

One way we like to keep track of books we read during an author study is to start an ongoing list. Students look forward to seeing the list grow as new titles are entered, and even students of early grades can be involved in maintaining the chart. This may also be a good time to learn about using capital letters for writing book titles.

Both individual and class charts can track the development of a study, highlighting award-winning titles with stars, ribbons, or some other symbol. We sometimes like to reorder the list at the end of a study and create a listing of books as they were published, also using this as an opportunity to learn about copyright dates. Sometimes, patterns about an author's work schedule emerge through this type of list. For example, when we reordered a list of books by Peter Catalanotto, we realized that he illustrates a book by another author and writes and illustrates one of his own each year.

WONDERINGS AND GUESSES

As readers we naturally begin to wonder and make predictions about our reading. Reading another book by an author that is familiar to you may lead you to wonder if the author is going to use similar techniques in this book, too. Modeling your own authentic responses after a shared reading can stimulate lively discussions of student wonderings. For instance, you might let students know that after reading Judith Viorst's *The Goodbye Book*, you couldn't help but wonder if this story was based on one of her own sons, as some of her other books are. You could take it further and make a guess that it was inspired by many experiences Viorst must have had as a mother of three sons.

You can list these wonderings and guesses on a chart that keeps growing, giving direction and focus to the author study. Particular wonderings that keep coming up will drive the study, as with a fourth-grade class that wondered why Jean Fritz seems so consumed with American history. These wonderings and guesses led students to research Jean Fritz's memoirs, speeches, and biographical references, finally satisfying their curiousity.

Jean Fritz Author Study

Wonderings
- How does she get her information?
- Did she want to be a writer when she was young?
- What was her first book?
- How did she feel about getting published?
- Where does she get ideas for her books?

Guesses
* She probably reads a lot.
* Yes, because she's so good she must be doing it a long time!
* Homesick, because it's about her childhood
* She probably told everyone she knew because she felt proud.
* She could read other books, visit historical places and talk to people who know a lot.

COMPARING AND CONTRASTING BOOKS

Readers naturally compare books they have read by favorite authors. This is a strategy we would like our students to feel comfortable with. When first-grade students heard their teacher read *Dylan's Day Out* by Peter Catalanotto, they were able to discuss ways that this book was similar to Catalanotto's *Mr. Mumble*, which they were familiar with from an earlier readaloud.

Students working independently can compare books they are reading by an author to a book you are reading aloud by the same author. One way to capture this discussion on paper is to simply make a listing called "Both Books Have" and record similarities the children notice. Make a double entry list labeled "Similarities" on one side and "Differences" on the other. Venn diagrams are an excellent graphic organizer for these responses as well. Record similarities in overlapping sections of the circles and unique

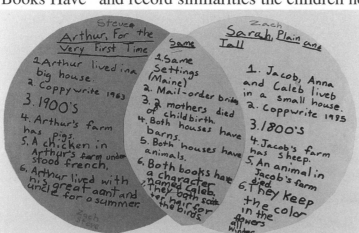

characteristics for each book in the circles designated by title. We have often used this technique, comparing and contrasting characters within a book, between books, or, even characters in a book and ourselves.

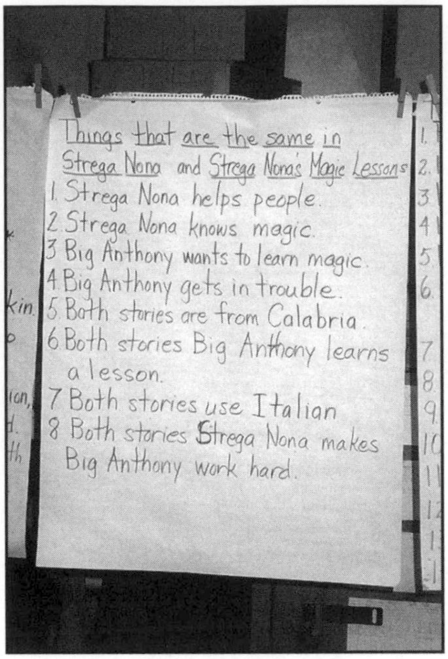

NOTICING AN AUTHOR'S STYLE

Once we have shared at least two or three of the author's books with our students and have made some comparisons, we are well on our way towards noticing things this author seems to do often. So it's no surprise that when a group of third graders saw that their teacher was going to read William Steig's *Brave Irene*, they responded as experts when asked what they expected to find inside the covers. They had already heard three of Steig's other books and anticipated that perhaps someone would get lost or there might be some magic at work. Their responses were recorded on a chart labeled "Things We Notice About William Steig's Style." After reading more Steig books and having time to talk within small groups about students' noticings, additional responses were recorded.

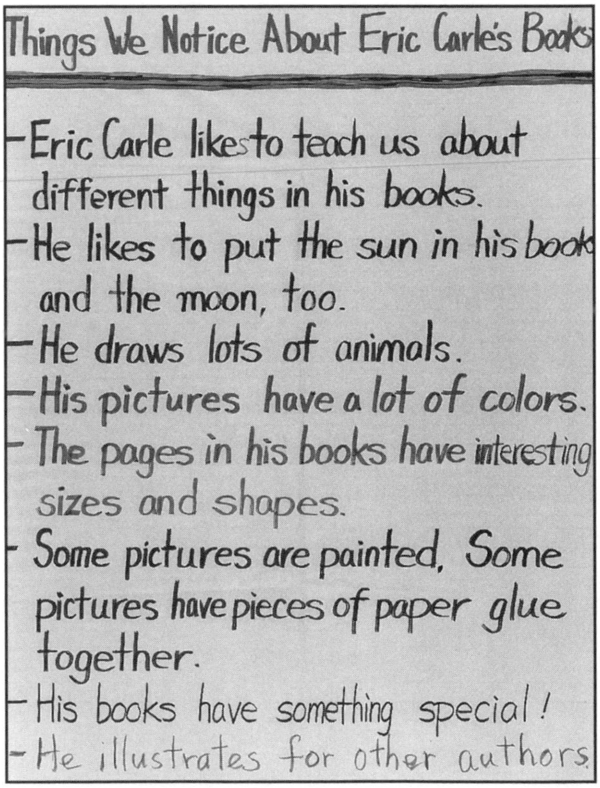

Students who are reading different books by the same author independently can keep track of noticings as they continue reading. Read alouds offer additional exposure to an author's work. Small-group discussions and share meetings provide opportunities to discover, support, and confirm noticings.

The chart in the photograph reads:

> Things that are the same in
> Strega Nona and Strega Nona's Magic Lessons
> 1. Strega Nona helps people.
> 2. Strega Nona knows magic.
> 3. Big Anthony wants to learn magic.
> 4. Big Anthony gets in trouble.
> 5. Both stories are from Calabria.
> 6. Both stories Big Anthony learns a lesson.
> 7. Both stories use Italian
> 8. Both stories Strega Nona makes Big Anthony work hard.

The chart labeled reads:

> Things We Notice About Eric Carle's Books
>
> - Eric Carle likes to teach us about different things in his books.
> - He likes to put the sun in his books and the moon, too.
> - He draws lots of animals.
> - His pictures have a lot of colors.
> - The pages in his books have interesting sizes and shapes.
> - Some pictures are painted, Some pictures have pieces of paper glue together.
> - His books have something special!
> - He illustrates for other authors

CONNECTIONS TO BIOGRAPHICAL INFORMATION

Earlier we discussed some places and ways to research biographical information and now we'll look at how to use it. Sometimes this information is available in the author center in our classrooms, inviting curious young readers to investigate on their own by reading or listening to taped interviews. Another way we like to share biographical information is by telling amusing anecdotes or relevant information at appropriate times during the author study.

For instance, when reading *The Snowy Day* by Ezra Jack Keats, we shed light on the author's inspiration for the character of Peter by sharing the story Keats often told about the photograph he ripped from a *Life* magazine and hung on his wall for several years of a little black boy whose uplifted face was beautiful to him. That picture eventually became Peter's story. Sharing anecdotes works well for readers of all ages and especially for those too young to read biographical sketches on their own. For independent readers, make copies of the information for groups to read and share and create charts titled "Things We Know About (Author)." As readers discover new information, the chart grows. Published biographies or autobiographies are wonderful sources of information, whether they're read aloud in their entirety or as appropriate excerpts, or read independently. You can introduce video- and audiotapes the same way.

Children often react with a genuine look of *aha!* as they are able to make connections between biographical information and the work of an author. When fifth graders studying Roald Dahl's books noticed that several of his teacher characters are quite negatively portrayed, they naturally wondered why he does this. After the teacher read several chapters in *Boy*, Dahl's autobiographical work, they connected his traumatic experiences in boarding school to the characters he created.

Mini-lessons and share sessions can help formalize these connections. A young colleague of ours taught us a technique of using color-coded markers to highlight a chart entitled "Connections Between Author's Life and Writing." Write the word *life* in one color and the word *writing* in another. Record a relevant piece of biographical data in one color and then the connected evidence from the writing in the second. Once again, this is a chart that develops over the course of an author study and is an integral activity that brings the author to the students as a mentor for their own writing.

CATEGORIZING BOOKS

One of the things students notice after reading books by Paul Fleischman is that he writes in several genres. In studying authors who write in more than one genre, students might categorize the books by listing titles under headings such as *Poetry, Short Stories, Picture Books, Nonfiction,* and so on. A kinder-garten class categorized Tomie dePaola's books, including autobiographical, nonfiction, folk stories, and other genres among his prolific collection, by placing them in color-coded baskets during the study.

ATTRIBUTE CHARTS

A great way to compare books and sum up a study is to create an attribute chart. Students can begin by identifying techniques particular to the author being studied. A group of first graders, after hearing the books read aloud and noticing the things Eric Carle seems to do frequently in his books, kept track of animal characters, special design effects, repeating phrases, and other attributes. Their chart indicated a *yes* or *no* in the appropriate spaces. As a study progresses, students can contribute information about the attributes for each of the book titles, recording additions as more books are shared.

GRAPHING RESPONSES TO BOOKS

We're always interested in finding authentic ways to make connections between content areas. Author studies naturally lead to math activities such as categorizing books by genre, reordering books by copyright dates, and graph-

STYLE	The Mitten	The First Dog	The Trouble With Trolls	Berlioz The Bear
Illustrations	• She puts a border around every page • pictures are in the borders • the borders tell what happens next - you can predict ⇒ FORESHADOWING • uses a lot of white, brown, blue, green & red	• borders helped us predict - foreshadow • some borders showed what the dog was talking about • uses a lot of brown, green and purple	• uses borders to show action • we think she used paints • she used a lot of red, green & white • deep colors - nature	• Foreshadowing borders • Lot's of detail in illustrations
Characters	• boy named Nicki • grandmother - Baba • a lot of animals... mole, rabbit, hedgehog, owl, fox, bear, mouse	• animals as characters - dog • child as character • characters faced a troubled situation	child - Treva dog (like the dog in The First Dog	• isn't human - b Berlioz • each time one othe came to do somethi The First Dog, The M Annie and the Wild t • A lot of animals - be bunnies, dog, hedge
Language	• repeats phrases (quickly moved over/ safe and sound) • cumulative tale • folk tale (genre)	• repeats phrases (he listened to the left and he listened to the right)		• Things keep repeat animals get more o hole.
Story Problem & Solution	• Nicki loses his mitten • animals need a place to come in from the snow • all the animals go in mitten • mitten gets found when animal sneezes and mitten flys to sky		• trolls keep wanting to take Treva's dog - so she has to keep giving them her things instead of dog! • she tricks the trolls into giving her back her things when they want her to show them how to fly on skis	• Bears can't get orchestra because is stuck in hole won't go! • Bee stings m he moves, wheel o hole. Similar to The M mouse solved th

ing. At the end of a study, students can vote on favorite titles or characters, then tabulate and graph results. One fifth-grade ESL (English as a Second Language) teacher we know taught her class many kinds of graphs as part of several author studies throughout the school year, extending the response pool by reading the author's work and polling students in other classes.

WRITING TO AN AUTHOR

It is so exciting to receive an author's response to students' letters (See postcard from Judith Viorst on page 44.) When you see children's faces as you read the letter aloud, you'll realize that the author has become someone very real and important to them. We urge you to make time for students to write to the authors you study; however, we suggest that you make it optional. Not every student feels compelled to do this, but students who are particularly taken with an author you study could be encouraged to write a letter.

Often we model the process of writing to an author first in a mini-lesson and allow readers time to talk together, rehearsing their ideas before writing their letters. Authors sometimes write letters to their readers on the inside covers of book club brochures and these might serve as models, too. This is the time to remind students that it's not a good idea to ask questions that they already know the answers to. But it is a good idea to request clarification about something that you know. Readers will want to communicate their favorites, their noticings and connections, and their wonderings and guesses. We also like to give writers opportunities to share first drafts with partners and their class community. Positive comments from other writers and specific ideas for improving their writing help raise the quality of the letters.

When the letters have been revised, mini-lessons might focus on editing skills, with time for peers to co-edit and teachers to confer with individual students. This is a great opportunity for purposeful letter writing and finding out about postal procedures! Most letters to authors can be sent in care of their publisher(s) and will usually be forwarded. If possible, let students find out the correct addresses for the publishers and contact-persons' names. Some of the resource books we recommended for biographical information list addresses of featured authors (see page 130). Students can participate in calculating the cost of sending the letters, purchasing stamps, and mailing them.

> Dear Mr. carlle :
> I like your books.
> you are a book man.
> I Love The very busy spider.
> I like to read your books.
> your pictures are nice.
> The spider book has spider web.
> On The very busy spider book the
> spider is very big.
> Are you very old now? because you
> write so many books already.
>   William

We sometimes send a bunch of letters to an author with an accompanying note from all of us letting them know something about the class and suggesting that a single letter to the class would be quite welcomed. If you are fortunate enough to have a personal connection to an author, this will make a response more likely. (For more on contacting authors, see page 133.) Although authors have infrequently disappointed us, the risk of this happening is minimal and worth taking based on our experiences. Most often children will get a response of some kind, perhaps a personal one from the author, or sometimes a packet from the publicist who handles mail for authors who can't deal with large volumes of letters. When we do get a return letter, we proudly share it with other classes by displaying it not only in our room but by posting a copy in the hallway as well. We are delighted that so many creative and busy authors take the time to answer their fan mail and make a lasting impact.

> Dear Kids –
> Thanks for writing. It was great to hear from you. This is a photo album where I live & write my books.
>   Your friend
>   Judith Viorst
> P.S. Read books! A book can be as delicious as a hot fudge sundae + as exciting as a ride on a rollercoaster.

> Class of
> P. Hornstein (201)
> P.S. 321
> 180 7 ave
> Brooklyn, NY 11215

TEXT INNOVATIONS

Young writers who are very familiar with an author's work are comfortable building on the author's ideas. The books provide a scaffold for students to successfully create their own writing. Books that have a repeating pattern are perfect for innovations. Many teachers create sentence frames based on a book and encourage students to make changes. For example, students can change one segment, such as "Brown bear, brown bear, what do you see?" to "Green frog, green frog, what do you see?" More sophisticated writers might create innovations by changing the character, the setting, the beginning, the problem, the ending, or the point of view. You might model your own innovations to demonstrate the process of deciding what to change.

Students can work with partners or in small groups to decide what to change and then recreate the text, building on the author's use of patterns and designing their own illustrations. Arnold Lobel's characters of Frog and Toad are perfect for creating innovations. Students know their personalities so well, they love to create original adventures for them. We've seen students experiment with settings, problems, beginnings and endings to successfully create text innovations. Innovations can be published as class big books or as individual books.

Many authors have admitted that they began their own writing careers by imitating favorite authors. What we used to think of as copying, we now understand is a framework for creative writing, and we encourage writers to mimic authors to gain mastery of the process of writing. We recognize this small step toward originality as the beginning of the student's feeling of authorship. As students experience success in their innovations, they naturally assume more responsibility for their decisions as authors and are willing to take greater risks. We find that these tentative beginnings lead to independence, competence, and confidence.

CELEBRATING AUTHOR STUDIES

Many students and teachers agree that celebrations are the best part of an author study, for they acknowledge the beginning of the journey of discovery but not necessarily the end. Students often continue to study—and celebrate—an author long after the celebration has ended as new books become available. Celebrations bring a satisfying conclusion and document discoveries which become part of a classroom's literary history. They are also a lovely way to involve the school community and parents. Students can be responsible for creating guest lists, designing invitations and programs, and setting timetables. Here are some ideas for culminating your author studies:

Here's to Ann Cameron!

• Thanks for bringing Julian to life.
• Thanks for making us laugh with Huey.
• Your words will stay with us.
• Keep writing about Julian.
• Your book about the most beautiful place made us think about our beautiful places.
• Good luck in Guatamala.
• Thanks for teaching us how to use beautiful language.

Toast to the author. Our students love to acknowledge the pleasures an author has given them by lifting their cups of juice and toasting! We often start off by modeling an appropriate toast and then invite students to take over. We like to record the toasts on chart paper. You might like to give students time to think about their toast for homework or during small-group discussions.

Books about the author. Students might like to write books about the author using information they have researched and discovered during the study. We've seen some beautiful big books made by binding together all of the charts generated throughout a study. Students like to enhance the charts with illustrations and photographs taken during various author-study activities.

Sharing favorites.

Students can select favorite books or passages to read aloud. A mini-lesson that explores effective read-aloud techniques is helpful, followed by time to practice reading aloud, which builds fluency and confidence. Build in success by encouraging students and family members to coach and support each other. You might schedule readings over a weeklong in-class celebration or invite students to sign up to share their favorites by visiting other interested classes in the school. Many teachers we know take this opportunity to make audio- and videotapes that become part of the author-study collection.

Choral readings. Some of the authors we study write books that have refrains, repetitions, and rhythmic language, enticing students to jump into choral readings. Students with limited English proficiency (LEP) especially benefit from and enjoy this kind of celebration. The class can help decide how best to chorally read a book, experimenting with possibilities. Bill Martin, Jr.'s, books are fun for choral reading.

Drama presentations. Turning a favorite book or chapter into a play is a wonderful, purposeful activity requiring rereading and careful reflection. Students choose the author's work they want to dramatize,

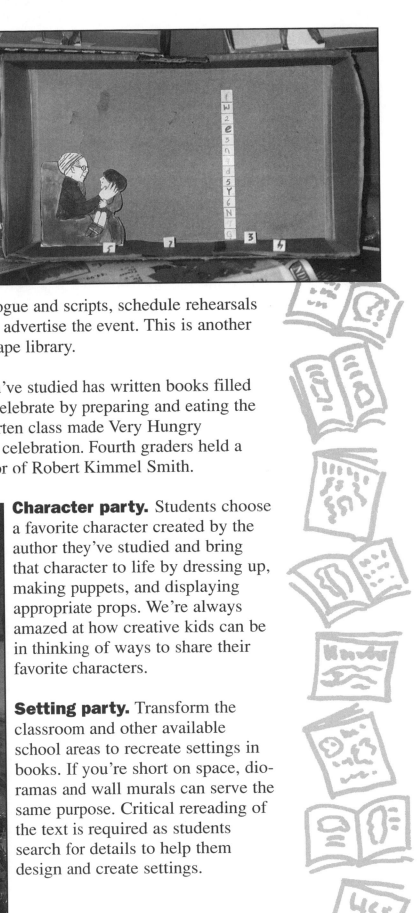

decide on roles and props, work on dialogue and scripts, schedule rehearsals and performances, and design posters to advertise the event. This is another chance to add to your audio- and videotape library.

Food party. Sometimes the author you've studied has written books filled with references to food, and it's fun to celebrate by preparing and eating the foods mentioned in the text. A kindergarten class made Very Hungry Caterpillar Fruit Salad for an Eric Carle celebration. Fourth graders held a jelly bean and chocolate festival in honor of Robert Kimmel Smith.

Character party. Students choose a favorite character created by the author they've studied and bring that character to life by dressing up, making puppets, and displaying appropriate props. We're always amazed at how creative kids can be in thinking of ways to share their favorite characters.

Setting party. Transform the classroom and other available school areas to recreate settings in books. If you're short on space, dioramas and wall murals can serve the same purpose. Critical rereading of the text is required as students search for details to help them design and create settings.

Interviews. Students can team up to prepare their own audio and video interviews, with one student playing the part of an author or character and the other acting as reporter. Students can use information they've gathered during the study to prepare questions and answers. Add transcripts of these interviews to your author-study collection.

Art activities. There is no limit to art activities inspired by author studies. We've seen beautiful quilts commemorating all the characters created by Tomie dePaola, little chairs modeled after Vera B.

Williams's *A Chair for my Mother*, and wild hats to compete with the one Ezra Jack Keats designed for Jennie! Let your students' imaginations and an author's inspiration lead you to more creative art extensions.

Music and movement activities. Many children excel in and enjoy expressing themselves through music and dance. Translating prose into movement and song and creating original musical pieces and dances are just some of the ways students can celebrate a joyful author study.

Chapter

5

Teaching Skills and Strategies

It's not surprising that teachers at all stages of experience are concerned about literacy skills. While some of us wonder which skills are supposed to be taught and when, others are thinking about appropriate techniques for reinforcing the skills. Skills do have a place in a literature-based approach to learning; in fact, it is within the context of real reading and writing that skills are most meaningfully acquired and internalized as regularly used strategies.

Mini-lessons and discussions that focus on skills don't interfere with the pleasure of reading and responding to the literature because the focus comes from the literature itself as well as the needs and interests of the readers. For example, students who are about to read a very descriptive setting passage could be encouraged to focus their attention on the words the author chooses to create a strong image of place and time. A teacher who is about to read aloud a chapter that is loaded with events relevant to the plot might ask her students to listen for the particular sequence of events. When skills are taught and practiced for purposeful, authentic reasons, students tend to apply the skills in other situations on their own. Noticing our students as they read and write assures us of their ability to successfully decide when and how to use skills and demonstrates that they are in control of using the skills as strategies for their own purposes.

Author studies provide a framework for encouraging readers to use skills and develop strategies to enhance responses to authors and books. This chapter defines and describes some of these techniques, including predicting, webbing, story mapping, listing, chunking, relationship mapping, using context, dialoguing, and reacting entries. You can use the techniques to respond to individual books or chapters during an author study, or perhaps as a way to summarize relationships between several books by a particular author. We find these techniques and activities have appeal for the following reasons:

•◆ They provide an organization that invites written response for all levels of readers and writers. The open-ended format encourages both emergent and fluent readers and writers to respond and feel successful.

•◆ They are generic formats that can be used for most books at appropriate times. Once you and your students become comfortable with the techniques, choice of response format can be personal preference, which empowers students and acknowledges their ability to make decisions.

•◆ They are a written documentation of skill development. The opportunity to look through students' response notebooks, or a collection of class charts, and see how their responses have grown over time is a valuable assessment tool.

It's likely that you will want to model the techniques during skills mini-lessons that are tailored to your students' needs and interests during an author study. If you're sharing a read-aloud with the whole class, you or a student can record responses on chart paper. For group work, students can be responsible for recording responses on charts, sharing discoveries later in the whole-class meeting. If students are working independently, you might want to model the techniques first in a mini-lesson by using a single book by the author, then send students off to investigate their own books. Students can also record reactions in their own reading response notebooks and share entries during small-group and whole-class share time.

The techniques and activities, some of which may be familiar to you, are described here as they might be used in an author study.

PREDICTING

Good readers make predictions throughout their reading. Readers often use this skill when they choose books to read, as they look at the covers, skim the pages, or read the blurbs on the back covers. We like to model this skill often during reading because we hope that young readers will make it part of their reading strategies.

Predictions About _Felita_ by Nicholasa Mohr

Guesses	Reasons	Evidence
It's about a girl.	The title is a girl's name. The cover illustration shows 3 girls.	The story is told through Felita's eyes. p.13 "Right up until that very moment I didn't believe it would happen.
The girl is probably Latina	The author's other book was about a Latino family.	p.15 "Mami" "Papi" "Paquito" "Consuela"
The girl will have a hard time.	The back blurb says she has to move + gets teased in her new neighborhood. In the Table of Contents, ch. 2 is "Trouble"	p.35 " , eah, there's none of your kind here and we don't want you."
She lives in a city.	The inside illustrations look like a city.	p.15 "Boy I loved my block, I knew just about everybody on this street."
Everything will be fine in the end.	Ch. 6 is "Making Up"	p.100 "It was just like before, only better." surprise! p.109 "My abuelita died at the end of spring."

There are many contexts for its use and many written formats to document predictions. We encourage students to make guesses and explain their reasons; they follow through by gathering evidence from the reading to see how well their guesses stand up. Before you formally read the book, ask students to make guesses based on the title, cover illustration, familiarity with the author's work, table of contents, back cover blurb, dedication, and a quick look at the inside. Chart guesses and reasons, then add a third column to record evidence as the book is read.

Students can use this skill during suspenseful parts of a book, too. Sometimes we make predictions prior to reading the book by generating questions, either based on the parts of the book mentioned previously or once again at the right moment in the book. The questions are just another way to get readers to connect to the book through their predictions. We often list the predictions on chart paper during the mini-lesson, add to them during further discussions, and keep them accessible throughout the study so readers can refer to them. When readers use this skill often, noting details and inferring, they are increasing their book awareness.

SEMANTIC MAPPING OR WEBBING

Webbing is an organizational technique for graphically illustrating responses to characters, authors' styles, settings, choice of words and use of language, themes, and more. Relationships between these factors become clear to readers as they develop a web. We sometimes provide the basic issues for a web during a mini-lesson and send our students off to research the top-

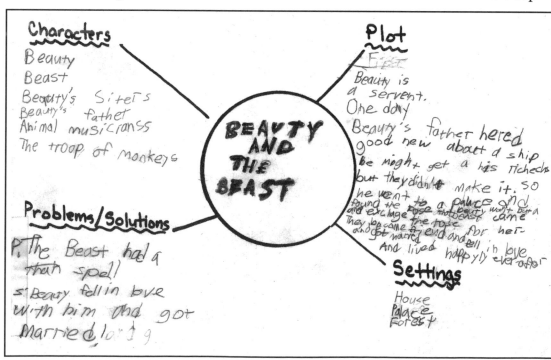

ics during reading and response group time. As students become more familiar with the technique, we encourage them to develop their own webs around issues that are of particular interest to them. During share time, students share what they've come up with, and we always invite students to add to their own webs then. We also use this time to collect responses and add to the web that we started during the mini-lesson, often facilitating connections and relationships between responses. When students build webs, they are collecting details, connecting them to main ideas, making word associations, categorizing, and applying prior knowledge to their reading.

VENN DIAGRAM

Although many of us remember first learning about Venn diagrams during math lessons, they are also a great technique for comparing and contrasting two or more issues in response to a reading. We have used Venn diagrams to compare and contrast issues from the same book, such as characters, or issues from a couple of books by the same author, such as setting or language. Readers record common elements in the overlaps between circles and write responses particular to designated circles in the remaining area.

male
4 sisters
doesn't seem close
    to his parents
really wants to
    win
shy
lots of TV
poor
likes to draw
    fearful

like running
same class
    at school
share Terabithia

female
only child
fastest
no TV
has money
faces her fears
not a typical girl
tomboy
good imagination

Jesse   Leslie

We sometimes give our students blank Venn diagram forms to use at first and define the circles during mini-lesson time, building in choice when appropriate. For example, we might begin a mini-lesson by asking students to contribute to a list of characters created by Paula Fox. We could then take two characters from the list and model a Venn diagram by setting up the circles and asking students for suggestions. Students are then invited to make their own Venn diagrams using any other two characters or going further with the ones already started. In addition to providing meaningful reasons for comparing and contrasting, students are also collecting pertinent details and categorizing them when they work with Venn diagrams.

STORY MAPS OR STORY GRAMMAR

We like this generic format to help students graphically explore the key elements of a story. When students fill in story maps (charts listing title, author, characters, settings, problems, events, solutions, etc.), either after completing readings or over time for longer readings, the structure and design of the stories become clear. Many students use story maps for their own writing as well.

We have used story maps to introduce important terms such as *problem, climax, goal, event,* and *setting.* We've had great discussions about which char-acters should be listed in each section of a story map and have often used this teachable moment to introduce major and minor character designation, even with very young readers.

Sometimes we use simplified versions of a story map depending on the age and level of the readers initially, using questions at times to provide more support. In any case, you may want to model a story map first for readers of all ages and levels by using a picture book read-aloud that is strong on plot, such as *Something Special For Me* by Vera B. Williams. William Steig's books also are strong problem/resolution examples. Certain elements of a story map can be introduced after reading a few chapters of a longer book. Or you might just read until the problem is laid out, then complete the sec-tions students know. You could even use the rest of the story map to make predictions or fill them in as they develop. This technique is flexible and incorporates many skills, such as identifying details, stating main ideas, sequencing, and inferring. It's interesting to look at several story maps in an author study to notice patterns or innovations in an author's writing style.

LISTS

Both of us make lists to keep track of the many things in our lives that we need to do. We realize that this is a technique that is also appealing to children because it is so doable. In addition to lists that we mentioned earlier in discussions about activities and strategies in an author study (things we notice about style, biographical information, etc.), we often suggest that stu-dents use lists to respond to their reading and to help with their writing.

Story Map

title: The Amazing Bone

author: William Steig

characters: Pearl*   the bone*   villains
            the fox*   parents   (* major characters)

setting: begins in a town   fox's house
         moves to a forest   Pearl's house

problem: Pearl's life is threatened by the fox.

events: 1. Pearl discovers the magic bone.
        2. The highway robbers threaten her, but the bone saves her.
        3. The fox captures Pearl and the bone and plans to eat them.
climax 4. The bone uses magic to shrink the fox to "the size of a mouse."
        5. Pearl goes home and the bone becomes part of the family.

solution: The bone realized that it could use magic.

Lists can have single or multiple headings and can be maintained over several reading sessions. Studying a particular author will generate lots of ideas for list headings. For example, in a Roald Dahl author study, fourth graders couldn't help but notice Dahl's use of made-up words in many of his books, which inspired many of them to start a list of these words.

We usually introduce possible headings for a list during a mini-lesson based on students' needs and the particular book and author. Students explore the topic during reading and response group time, make their lists in their reading response notebooks during writing time, and then share their lists during share time. Students can expand on their lists during discussions, both in their notebooks and on the chart introduced in the mini-lesson.

Some students like to stick to list-making for a while, and that's all right, but we gently coax them from one-word list entries to more detailed list entries, and finally to experimenting with other means of responding, such as webbing. Here are some other examples of lists that students kept during various author studies.

◆ Collect samples of a particular language technique used by an author, such as Ann Cameron's beautiful phrases.

◆ Keep a list of characters created by an author, such as Beverly Cleary, perhaps reorganizing the list under title headings or character traits.

◆ List descriptive words used by an author, such as Katherine Paterson, to help children see how an author creates images.

◆ List rhyming words found in books by Dr. Seuss and other authors who use this technique.

> **Ann Cameron's Beautiful Language**
>
> **Julian, Secret Agent**
> "It was a morning when the sun stayed in bed."
>
> "It was a morning when the clouds had pillow fights."
>
> "This is like living in an aquarium!"
>
> "He had muscles every place on his body that you could have and he looked mean."
>
> **Julian, Dream Doctor**
> "My dad is a quick moving man. When he runs he is fast as fire."
>
> "My mom is like a cool green planet with forests and flowers and waterfalls."
>
> "Anyplace around her is a good place to be."
>
> **The Stories Julian Tells**
> "When he laughs, the sun laughs in the windowpanes."
>
> "It will taste like a whole raft of lemons. It will taste like a night on the sea."
>
> "When he thinks, you can almost see his thoughts sitting on all the tables and chairs."

◆ Collect references to things that are familiar to the young readers of Judy Blume's books to point out one way of writing for a particular audience.

◆ List the kinds of clues mystery writers such as James Howe use in their books.

➥ Keep track of the sophisticated words that William Steig uses in his picture-book texts and notice how meaning is made clear to readers.

CHUNKING

Many readers, like ourselves, like to take some time to reflect when they finish a book. Particularly with books that are well liked, readers often say that they need some time to let the book live with them and sink in. Some of the response activities we've described foster this reflection about the book as a whole. Chunking is one more activity that works well at the end of a book.

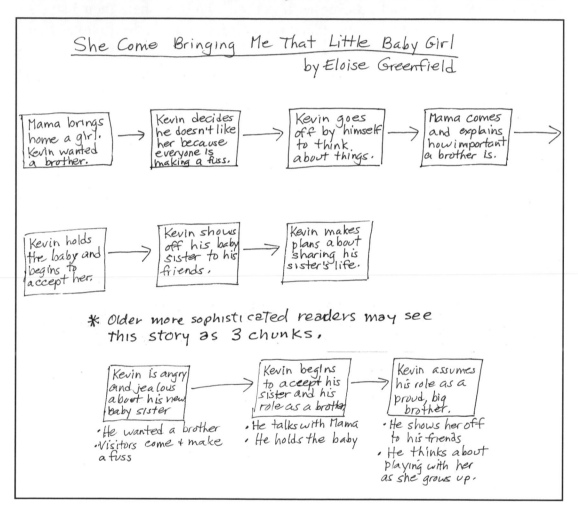

Chunking is just what it sounds like—looking at the story in a book and clustering or chunking events or ideas together. Some picture books work well as models for chunking. *She Come Bringing Me That Little Baby Girl* by Eloise Greenfield comes to mind. In chunking, it's not the little details that become chunks, but the cluster of details, or even main ideas, that we group together. Students might identify a chunk with a sentence that sums up what the chunk is about. Sometimes a single word or phrase will do. Some chunks reflect the plot, or reveal an author's decisions about the structure of the book.

Some teachers like to chunk out a book horizontally, others vertically. Either way, you can add the smaller details that flesh out each chunk. Chapter books are interesting to chunk because sometimes a single chapter is a chunk by itself, and other times a cluster of chapters makes up a chunk. Chunking reveals literary essentials such as turning points, character, setting, and mood changes. The technique builds in practical application of sequencing skills, supporting main ideas with details, and classifying. Chunking several books by an author can shed light on the author's choices about structure and encourage students to think about choices in their own writing. Small groups can each chunk a book and then compare discoveries during a share meeting.

RELATIONSHIP MAPS

Readers can use this technique with books that have character dynamics that call out for further study. We like to use this technique because it helps students dig deeper into the essence of characters and highlights authors' strategies for bringing characters to life. You might model the technique with a picture book that has strong character relationships or use a chapter book that the class is familiar with.

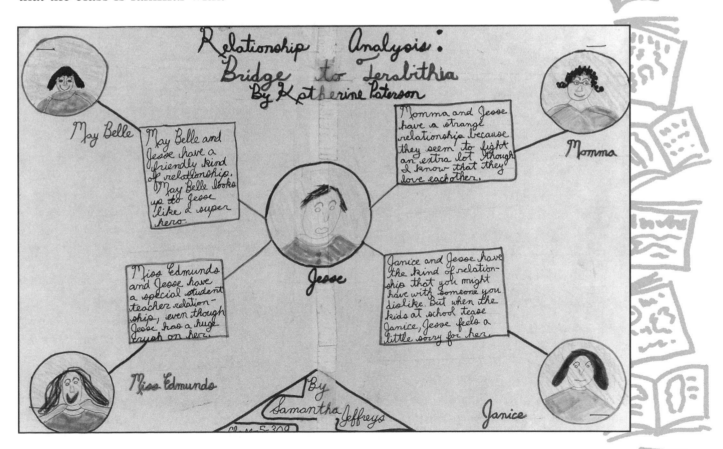

We introduce the technique during mini-lessons by asking students to contribute character names to a list. We examine the list, look for pairs or even trios of names that form relationships, and record the names on either side of double-sided arrows, signifying that the dynamics of the relationships are impacted by all the characters involved. We then ask students to share what they know about the relationships, adding these suggestions to the map. Sometimes we simply list all suggestions underneath the names, and other times we organize the details of the relationships under and over the names according to dynamics between the characters.

Students continue by developing their own relationship maps, selecting another pair of characters from the list or from another book by the same author. Groups could form around choice of books or character pairs. Some readers respond by noting details of relationships, then making inferences about the dynamics. Others begin to understand how and why authors juxtapose characters and introduce conflicts in their writing. This technique will

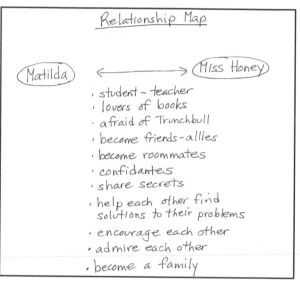

inevitably spark some very lively and sophisticated discussions during share time, inspiring many students to create more revealing relationship maps.

CONTEXT

Successful readers often derive word meaning from the context of the reading material. You can model this skill for students and encourage them to make it their own strategy through meaningful context application.

We like to apply this skill during mini-lessons with real situations, taking words in context from students' reading. William Steig's picture books provide wonderful ways to develop this strategy with students because the text is filled with sophisticated vocabulary words surrounded by contextual clues. You might consider reading aloud a Steig book such as *Sylvester and the Magic Pebble* as part of an author study. After reading a second or third Steig book, students will notice the author's use of "hard words." This is the perfect opportunity for a mini-lesson on context clues. During a second reading of *Sylvester and the Magic Pebble*, you could ask students to listen for some of those hard words and record them on a chart. Ask students to guess the meaning of the words and share reasons for their guesses. By doing this, students teach each other strategies for using context rather than relying on the teacher for "the way."

We have also put passages from Steig's books on overhead transparencies or chart paper to visually bring the text to all the students. To make it even more concrete, we write a single word on a piece of construction paper or a transparency and ask students to guess the meaning. Because the word is isolated, students usually suggest that we use a dictionary. We acknowledge that that would be a good idea, then we ask if students could find the meaning if they saw how the word is used in the story. We put the word into a sentence by placing another sheet of construction paper, or a second transparency, over the word. This sheet has a sentence, or a passage, with a space cut out so that the word fits into the context. Again students guess the meaning and share the clues they used. We record the guesses, then consult the dictionary for confirmation. We record the strategies for using context on a chart and keep it available to refer to for students. The chart could be called "How (William Steig) Helps Us With Vocabulary."

Depending on the needs of your students, you might decide to further explore each of the suggested context strategies during other mini-lessons. Encourage students to use the strategies during their own reading and during conferences, read alouds, and so on.

DIALOGUING THROUGH LETTERS

Informal letterwriting is a natural transition from oral to written language because it allows writers to retain their natural voices. You don't have to write like anyone else to get your point across when responding to literature in a letter to another reader. We like to use letterwriting because it is authentic and purposeful.

You can start written dialogues by writing to your students and inviting responses. This first letter serves as a stimulus and as a model of the possibilities for letterwriting, in terms of form and content. In an author-study context, the letter could include wonderings about an author, reactions to books or characters, or plans about continuing the author study. It's a good idea to end the letter with an open-ended question that could get students started on a response.

Many teachers are concerned about the number of letters they would have to respond to with this activity. Some teachers we know write individual letters back after one or two rounds of responses, then switch over to class letters with a copy for each student. You could also consider having students continue the dialogue through letters with each other. One teacher we know designed an entire author study around a written dialogue that included letters between students and the teacher, letters between students, from students to the author, and to characters in the books. Another colleague asked students to choose one of the characters created by an author and write letters as that character might. The students formed dialogue pairs and corresponded with each other in character.

Dear Jessie,

When Leslie died, you must have felt devastated. I feel sorry for you. I felt sad when Leslie died too. Maybe you can find someone as good, imiginative, and a fast runner too. Well at least you have memmories of her. That can help sometimes. If it makes you feel better I lost a friend too. I couldn't even go to the funeral.

From

Venus

Students can design their own stationery. If you're studying an author/illustrator, you may suggest using the illustrative style of the author for inspiration. The possibilities for using this format are endless, and students of all levels can participate successfully. We love to look at a series of letters that a student has written over a period of time because this affords a wonderful opportunity to watch for signs of growth and informs our teaching about the needs of our students.

REACTION ENTRIES

This response technique encourages readers to record multidimensional responses to their reading. This activity also opens up discussions about personal reading preferences and behaviors. In addition, it is one more opportunity to get students thinking, talking, and writing about their responses to the books they are reading. Some students stay with one key issue over time, while others dabble in several each day.

One fifth-grade class we worked with was reading books by Scott O'Dell. The teacher was interested in getting students to document their varied reactions to the many layers of O'Dell's work. For instance, she noticed that some students were excited about the factual and historical information they were getting from the literature, and others were reacting to the plot line and characters.

We suggested that she start off the next mini-lesson by sharing this observation with her students and asking them what other issues they were

Dear Ricardo,
How are you doing? I Just finished reading the book Chester Crickets pigeon ride. The book was very Interesting. my favorite character was Chester is a very energetic Incect. He is known for his chirping. In the book Chester meets a pigeon named Lu Lu. I highly recomend the book to anyone who like to read. Enjoy.

Sincerly,
Stephen

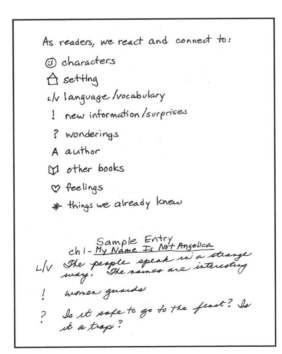

As readers, we react and connect to:

☺ characters
⌂ setting
L/v language /vocabulary
! new information /surprises
? wonderings
A author
📖 other books
♥ feelings
✳ things we already knew

Sample Entry
ch 1 - My Name Is Not Angelica
L/v The people speak in a strange way. The names are interesting

! women guards

? Is it safe to go to the feast? Is it a trap?

reacting to in the reading. They generated a list that included historical information, characters, plot, language, vocabulary, surprises, questions, things they already knew (prior knowledge), connections to other books, and connections to author information.

The next step involved designating a symbol for each of these reaction issues. The teacher then modeled the response process by 1) reading aloud a chapter from *My Name Is Not Anjelica*; 2) asking students to share responses with each other verbally in small groups and then in the large-class share meeting; and 3) recording their responses by putting the appropriate symbol in the margin and then jotting down a sentence or two for the response.

After collecting and recording a few different response entries, she called their attention to the varied responses readers can have to the same material. For the next couple of weeks, students responded to their reading using this format, enjoying the power of choosing their own issues for reading responses. Share sessions were very interesting as students discovered what their peers were noticing about the same material.

Chapter

6

Grouping for Author Studies:
A Sample Katherine Patterson Study

Study groups have been around since the days of the one-room schoolhouse—they allow one adult to work with large numbers of students who have varied needs and interests, while giving students the opportunity to learn from each other and create lasting relationships. Groups in the past, however, too often remained permanent. Fortunately for the students in our classrooms, we understand the necessity of varying the size, number, purpose, and duration of the groups we form.

The most important thing to remember in grouping for author studies is flexibility. Groups need time to learn to work together successfully. Some may work better than others. As you observe group interactions and reflect on your noticings, you'll want to take an active role in adjusting and fine-tuning group dynamics. Discussions of other considerations follow.

SIZE

Groups may have as many as six members or as few as two. Partners often are an excellent way to begin group work as it is usually easier to work with one other person than many. As students acquire communication skills, larger groups may form. You may decide on the ideal number of students in each group and the number of working groups by carefully considering the number of students in your class, the number of desks, available space, the number of multiple copies of books available, and the strategies your students demonstrate in cooperative learning.

ABILITIES

Teachers sometimes form groups of similar abilities in order to guide members through the reading process. Ability groups allow teachers to focus on skills and strategies, as well as on interests and needs. Because of the group's small size, individual attention and positive feedback are possible. Students benefit from reading with others at a similar pace without the pressure of keeping up with faster readers. Because they are at similar reading levels, they can share their strategies, support each other in creating meaning, and safely take risks.

Finding an author whose books are at a comfortable readability level enables students to use skills and strategies acquired through guided reading and apply them for their own purposes. Students independently build fluency and confidence when they read and reread many books at or below their reading level. We've seen remarkable growth in interest and ability occur when students are given time to stay with the books they choose to read. Too often, we tend to push our students to the next level before they've had time to meaningfully practice and incorporate skills and strategies necessary to truly feel competent.

SOCIAL ISSUES

People naturally tend to choose to associate with other people who are similar to them. Given opportunities to form their own groups, students often join together based on commonalities in personality, socioeconomic, ethnic, gender, or race factors. As the classroom leader, you may want to allow your students to form groups based on these considerations some of the time. However, because the best classroom communities encourage students to work with people who are different than they are, you'll also want to help students form diverse groups, combining, for example, introverted with outgoing or aggressive students with peace makers. A few ideas for forming diverse groups are to have students choose random cards, pick pieces of puzzles, or join in groups based on their birthdays. Students seem to accept this system as long as they know it is fair and of a limited duration.

Many teachers are committed to creating small-group experiences that encourage students to get to know each other during short-term interactions. The experiences students have in forming and working together in groups help them to make informed decisions and learn necessary skills in cooperation. Often these short-term interactions prepare students in forming groups that work successfully over long periods of time.

To ensure the best chance for success in group interactions, it is helpful to spend classroom time discussing strategies for working in groups. Students need time to think, talk, and write about qualities necessary for effective group interactions, potential problems and how to solve them, and roles of group members. Class discussions allow students to take control of the process and dynamics of group work and empower them to make informed decisions.

BOOKS

After hearing about an author's books from other readers and browsing through possible selections, students may choose their groups according to their interest in particular books. Of course, it's necessary that the selected books offered are on the appropriate reading level of the students to ensure a successful author study.

DURATION

You may want to keep groups together for as long as your author study progresses, so students have the chance to build rapport and trust over time. As groups begin to establish rules for behavior and expectations, members often begin to take more responsibility for decisions. They may choose to rotate each member's job, set their own daily and weekly agenda, and plan

projects and presentations to culminate their study. The most successful groups may serve as models for the others, sharing their process in decision making, secrets of success, and solutions to ongoing problems. You might even allow students to spend some time observing the function of these model groups to highlight successful strategies. Mini-lessons may focus on these observations to encourage other groups to adapt them for their own use.

We have found that some groups may not endure and may choose to disband them as soon as it becomes obvious that they are failing. The members may be reorganized or some may choose to join other functioning groups. Other times we may join the troubled group, modeling cooperative behavior and helping members to find effective ways to work together. The expectation that every student in the class must learn to work successfully in a group should be clear, yet at the same time we need to remain flexible about finding the best possible group for every class member.

A SAMPLE AUTHOR STUDY: Katherine Paterson

This Katherine Paterson author study illustrates the challenges, thinking process, and strategies involved in forming groups of readers working independently in a fifth-grade classroom. Entries from the teacher's journal give you a close-up view of the essence of this author study and can help you visualize how one teacher structured and managed groups of students reading different books by the same author. You will see how she struggles with trying to meet the diverse needs of her students, balancing the demands of reluctant as well as fluent readers.

ENTRY 1

Just finished reading the first four chapters of *Bridge to Terabithia* to the class. Wonderful discussions about making friends, feeling lonely, families... Kids seem to be absorbed in the book. The talks tell me that we're coming together and seeing each other differently with Katherine Paterson's help. I think I'm ready to let the kids go on their own—try reading together as partners. I'll continue the morning sessions on the rug with a mini-lesson, then let them read the chapter with kids they choose. I'll circulate and bring them together at the end for a share meeting.

Worry about the choices they'll make for partners. Better plan a mini-lesson on strategies for choosing partners. Tonight for homework I'll ask kids to make lists in their reading notebooks of things they look for in reading partners to prepare for discussion tomorrow.

Mini-lesson. Begin session with chart, "Things We Look for in a Reading Partner." As kids add to list, discuss qualities and potential problems.

> Things To Look for In A
> Reading Partner
>
> Someone who:
> * likes the same kind of books
> * reads at the same pace or
> * or is patient and willing to speed up, slow down or wait.
> * is willing to talk about their ideas, feelings + reactions
> * cooperates in a group
> * does their share of the work
> * completes assignments on time
> * won't waste time

Reading-Writing Activity. I'm afraid to let the kids make choices for their partners on the spot. It always seems somebody is left out or somebody is unhappy. Instead, after the mini-lesson, I'll ask the kids to go off and think about the qualities and write a letter to me with their three choices and reasons for choosing.

Share Meeting. Because I want to continue building the momentum with the book, I'm going to read the next chapter aloud. I want to involve more kids in the reading experience, so I'll invite them to read the dialogue and become the characters.

ENTRY 2

Amazed at how well the partners are working together. Most kids really thought carefully about the qualities from the mini-lesson. They chose well. Past three days the mini-lessons focused on issues that have come up: pacing, ways to read together, staying on task, and the noise level. Share meetings have been used for open discussions about problems and some noticings about the day's chapter.

Since kids are very connected to the main characters, I'm going to ask them to choose one and write diary entries in their notebooks for homework. Their writing will help me evaluate depth of understanding and appreciation of details.

* Need to think about C., N., D., R., S., L., F., B. Anyone else? They were quiet during the share meeting and seem to be struggling to focus on the text. Need to sit in with them tomorrow and look at their reading notebooks. How can I make sure this works for them?

ENTRY 3

Spending much of my time hopping from struggling pair to pair (four sets of readers). My presence seems to help them stay with what's happening in the book but I know it isn't enough. I could form a small group but—almost finished with the book—don't want to separate them from the rest of the class. Keep in mind for the next book. Mini-lessons have been focused on responses to the book and strategies readers use to figure out difficult words and make meaning from clues. Notebook entries are growing stronger—more full of details from text and stronger personal connections.

Strategies For Choosing The Right Book
- Read the blurb to find out what the book is about.
- Look at the title and cover illustration to see if it draws you in.
- See what reviewers have to say about the book - Did it win any awards?
- Talk to other readers about the book
- Look at the chapter titles to get an idea of the plot
- Skim through the pages
- Read some of the text
- Ask yourself - "Is this book a challenge, already read, a smooth comfortable fit?"

* Want to make the most of the ending. How?
** Kids love this book (so do I). Should we do an author study to keep the feeling alive?
*** GET BOOKS!!!

ENTRY 4

Finished the book yesterday. After reading the last word of the final chapter to the class, the silence that filled the classroom said everything. Many of us cried and it felt so right.

Managed to get multiple copies of *The Great Gilly Hopkins, The Master Puppeteer, Jacob, Have I Loved, Park's Quest, Lyddie, The Sign of the Chrysanthemum*. The excitement around the Katherine Paterson Author Study Center is building as the kids look at the books and talk about which book they'll choose to read.

Katherine Paterson Author Study

Title	How It Begins & How It Affects The Reader	Juxtaposed Characters	How It Ends and How It Affects The Reader
Jacob Have I Loved	- description of ferry ride + island (setting) - hooks reader by hinting at trouble between sisters.	twin sisters	· sisters lead independent lives · not a happy ending, but realistic
Lyddie	- action - bear - sets up the situation - danger! - worried about the family	Lyddie — Diana	· Lyddie becomes independent · very realistic - but surprising.
The Great Gilly Hopkins	· meet characters · know some of her problems	Gilly — Mrs. Trotter	· Gilly's dreams don't come true · real - you can't always have what you want · hope it works out for Gilly

Still worried about my struggling readers. *Gilly* seems like the easiest for them to manage, but how can I convince them to choose it? How will I support them through it?

*Need to do a mini-lesson tomorrow on strategies for choosing the right book. How do readers decide?

**Speak privately to my 8. Sell them *Gilly*!

ENTRY 5

Launched the author study today. Each kid gave me his/her three choices of books to read and I formed the groups. Had to make some changes to second choices because of behavior and personality issues but I think it will work. I have six groups with about five members in each. Decided to keep my eight with me—joined their *Gilly* group. Thankfully they were happy to have me and things went well—at least for today.

Plan to keep the structure consistent with the whole class focused on the same mini-lesson followed by time for reading and writing activity in groups and ending with a share meeting. Probably will take the first hour and a half of the morning but may have to do some writing in notebooks for homework if we run out of time.

Mini-lesson. *Using Bridge to Terabithia* as a model, the kids will explore how the author begins the book and how that choice affects the reader.

Reading-Writing Activity. Each group will read the beginning of their books and discuss their responses to the author's decision about how to begin. The notebook entry will reflect the group's discussion.

Share Meeting. Begin an author study attribute chart with the first column summarizing Katherine Paterson's technique for beginning her books. (Plan to continue attribute chart as study progresses—kids can decide on other columns.)

Things we're noticing about that *Does Well As A writer* Katherine Paterson's style

1. Her words are very sophisticated and powerful. They make us stretch ourselves as readers.
2. She uses the same settings. Japan, country,
3. Writes about child-parent relationship *fathers*
4. She builds her books up to a climax, by building in a tension.
5. Most of her books have a child as a central character.
6. Some of her books have a quest in them.
7. Some of her books have stressful sibling relationships.
8. A lot of her books have death.
9. Her books have catchy titles that are *connected to the story!*
10. Her central characters have support from others.
11. Writes in <u>strong</u> characters!

*Next mini-lesson focus on wonderings—begin ongoing lists in notebooks.

**Ask kids to find other books by Katherine Paterson for making a book basket. Books can be signed out for independent reading at home and in school.

ENTRY 6

My *Gilly* group is working!!! Usually I get these students started by reading aloud until I'm sure I have everyone hooked. Then they take turns reading to the group—sometimes by paragraphs or pages. Their favorite lately is reading aloud as reader's theater. As they read the dialogue, they are learning the purpose and meaning of punctuation, and each day their expression and fluency get better. Reading this way also seems to improve their comprehension—discussions are full of connections and strong opinions. The best part is that they are eager to bring their ideas from their small group to the whole-class share meetings.

How does Katherine Paterson do it?

Strong on Character

1. She puts characters into new situations
2. They have problems and their reactions to them are revealing.
3. The situations they're in are clear to us.
4. Uses lots of description.
   - details - appearance
   - thoughts - reveals their inner thoughts!
5. Uses realistic settings - lots of research.
6. Shows their better side.
7. Sometimes, she holds back info. about the character & that makes you interested.
8. Sometimes, there's another character for contrast, or the situation colors the character for us. (Juxtaposition)
9. Strong personalities.
10. She makes you like them - it starts with Katherine Paterson.
11. We can relate to the character
12. Her characters break stereotypes.
13. She uses universal themes - we can still relate.
14. Hardship - poverty, famine, war
15. Lost parents - stressful relationships
16. Shows opposite side of character; tough → soft; soft → tough
17. Builds "bridges" for characters to love each other.
18. "Bridges" → everyone has to cross his/her bridge to find out more about him/herself. Always more bridges
19. Fear - all main characters have to overcome fear of something

The other groups seem to be OK too—notebook entries are good and response during share meeting seem on target.

*How can I spend more time with the other groups without abandoning my *Gilly* group?

**How do I support independence and still actively teach?

ENTRY 7

Today's mini-lesson focused on things Katherine Paterson does well in her writing. Kids were incredible and came up with a long list. They noticed her ability to build strong characters and how she uses the differences to point out contrasting traits to the reader. I never thought they would come up with this but, since they did, I took the moment to teach the technique of juxtapositioning.

Mini-lesson. Using *Bridge to Terabithia* as a model, notice how the author uses this technique with the characters.

Reading-Writing activity. Each group will look for examples in their book and make a list of specific details in their notebook.

Share Meeting. Add column to attribute chart for character juxtaposition.

*Still spending most of my time with the *Gilly* group although they seem to be on task.

ENTRY 8

Left the *Gilly* group on their own for most of the activity time. Made sure they would be successful without me, first by focusing the mini-lesson on a concrete task of finding words that describe a character's feelings, thoughts, or attitudes that I was sure they could do independently. Second, because I was worried about them attempting a new chapter alone, took the time for everyone to reread, knowing they would benefit from the opportunity. Last, before I left them I made sure they knew what to do and were on their way. When I was sure they wouldn't notice my absence, I tiptoed away.

Spent time joining the *Lyddie* and *Park's Quest* groups. Observed their search and interactions and noticed their insights and grasp of the techniques for making characters come to life. I think they are ready to try to apply what they've noticed to their own writing.

So pleased with the *Gilly* group. They kept on task throughout the activity time and were vocal and involved during the share meeting.

*New Ritual—Katherine Paterson Read-Aloud Sign Up. Volunteers sign up to read their favorite parts from their independent reading book at the end of the day.

ENTRY 9

Katherine Paterson's presence has taken over the classroom. Watching her interviewed on the video and sharing her biographical information and book-club letters has really brought her to life. Kids are noticing connections between her life and her writing. Many have written to her and are eagerly waiting for her reply.

Most kids are creating characters strongly influenced by the author during writing time. Lots of attention to juxtapositioning, descriptive language, dialogue, and characters' internal thoughts.

Some groups are almost finished with their books and ready to choose another book. *Gilly* group reading strongly but slowly— more independent but still need my attention. Probably will finish only one book instead of two or more.

*Author study has been going strong for about a month. When and how to culminate?

ENTRY 10

Gilly group has one more chapter to read. They are longing for a happy ending but suspect the worst. Yesterday's mini-lesson focused on endings in Katherine Paterson's books. Great, heated discussion about readers' need to feel satisfied vs. authors' need

to write truthfully. I'm wondering how this discussion will affect their decisions about how to end their own stories.

Been giving the culmination a lot of thought. Decided, because everyone is so taken with the author's command of language, to end our study with Katherine Paterson's words. Each group will find and present powerful passages from their books. The celebration is scheduled for two weeks from now, hopefully enough time for every group to finish their books, search for their powerful passages, copy and frame the words, and practice their oral presentations.

*Who should we invite?
**Design invitations, programs.
***Plan refreshments.

ENTRY 11

What a tribute—I'm so proud! So glad we had an audience of parents to share this event with. Thanks to M.'s mother we have a video that documents our accomplishments. The toasts kids made to Katherine Paterson and each other were a wonderful ending to this event and convinced me that this author study has been so much more than just a reading experience. I've learned how valuable the power of rereading is—especially for kids in the *Gilly* group. I need to get them more books they can easily read without me. They need time to practice at their own pace. This author study has been full of surprises. Once again I've learned the need to listen, to watch, and to trust my students.

*What's next? Maybe kids can form groups by choosing different authors to study. Possibilities for the *Gilly* group: Patricia Reilly Giff, Louis Sachar, Ann Cameron, Johanna Hurwitz.

Chapter

7

Read-Aloud Author Studies:
A Sample Ed Young Study

ringing an author's words to life through read alouds opens doors to the joys of reading for all students. Read-aloud author studies also allow you to choose authors whose words may be above students' independent reading levels. Because text is read to them, students are free to listen to the language of the author, make personal connections, and create their own meaning. This successful interaction with books is particularly important for students who do not see themselves as readers and writers and are not able to independently create meaning from print. Presenting an author study this way encourages students to begin the process of becoming competent readers and writers.

Read-aloud author studies require only single copies of an author's books. Books can be introduced by reading the words aloud and following with a class discussion. Students can reread these books themselves later. Because they are already familiar with the stories, students can make further connections with the author and deepen understandings. Rereading in this way helps students develop independence in reading.

Read-aloud studies lend themselves to authors who write picture books. This genre is the perfect blend of pictures and text and is enjoyed by readers of all ages. Picture books offer particular success for struggling readers, who can use illustrations to create meaning while engaging with less demanding text. There are so many authors to choose from. A brief list follows:

Eric Carle   Donald Crews
Chris Van Allsburg   Aliki
William Steig   Verna Aardema
Arthur Yorinks

A SAMPLE PICTURE BOOK STUDY:
Ed Young

This is the story of a group of sixth graders and their read-aloud author study adventure. Because many of these students were recent immigrants to America with limited English, they had few successful experiences reading books in English. Most did not view reading and writing as joyful activities and did not independently pursue them as part of their own learning. Their teacher decided to launch a picture book study in order to provide more positive experiences with books and authors. Reading aloud would give the gift of books and connect students with the pleasure and excitement of reading.

Preparations began by setting up a center in the classroom, making folders for each student, and visiting the library to select a start-up collection of picture books. The first week of the study initiated a ritual morning read-aloud followed by time spent in a circle sharing noticings about illustrations, problems and solutions, personal connections, and so on. A clothesline hung across the ceiling held charts for recording these comments. Students also kept lists of favorite authors and books in their folders, including reasons for their choices. Although there was some initial concern among students that "picture books are for babies," growing enthusiasm quickly overtook any objections.

After morning readalouds and discussions, students were invited to choose books to reread with partners. Again, they discussed their noticings and made entries in their notebooks. Before long, students were volunteering to read their favorites aloud to the class. Often, the day ended with this activity.

Once students were more familiar with the genre and some picture book authors, they began to discuss possible authors for a study, finally selecting Ed Young, who shared the same heritage as many of the students and whose books appeared on many students' lists of favorites. Ed Young's art, combined with his words would guarantee students a lifelong love of the magic and beauty of books. Furthermore, because he shared the same immigrant experiences, studying his life and work would strengthen the bonds between author and reader, allowing Ed Young to become a mentor to these sixth graders.

Students chose partners and topics to explore, including:

- ➡ research about Ed Young's life
- ➡ Ed Young's style of illustrating
- ➡ connections between books
- ➡ spiritual meaning in Ed Young's books
- ➡ symbols in Ed Young's books
- ➡ Ed Young's dedications

The study was conducted over a period of six weeks, with about an hour devoted to the study twice a week. Each session began with the teacher using a read-aloud or open-ended question to encourage students to notice something about one of the topics, including successful strategies for investigating the topics. Partners would then spend the next 20 minutes reading and rereading, taking notes about noticings, and talking together about their process.

The teacher would facilitate, supporting and guiding students, listening to discussions, and noticing future mini-lessons. The session ended with groups sharing their discoveries. Often students chose to write their groups' findings on large chart paper that became part of the author study center.

At the end of the study, students decided to work together to create an original class picture book, titled **The Ed Young Story**. Everything they learned about picture books was used to create their own, with Ed Young's words, ideas, and decisions as a guide and inspiration.

It is our intention to bring you this author study in the voice of these students. Although the typing is ours, everything else—the words, the illustrations, and the design decisions (see pages 83-95)—belong to the students of class 6-2, P.S. 1, New York. We proudly present **The Ed Young Story**:

Dedicated to:

Ed Young

Thank you for coming to our school.
We love your books.
We hope you will come again.

One day at P.S. 1 in Chinatown, class 6-2 discovered **The Little Fur Family**. Everyone tried to go and grab it because it had fur on the cover. It was also funny. After we finished reading, it we talked about the author and her name was Margaret Wise Brown. The illustrator was Garth Williams. After reading that book we read many different kinds of picture books. We noticed all the different kinds of color they had. The words were printed big and almost everyone felt that picture books were for babies because most picture books don't have that many words. We started to bring in our own picture books. Our teacher and Mrs. Kotch brought in picture books too. As we kept on reading them, Mrs. Grabler and Mrs. Kotch decided to try and get Ed Young to visit us because we were so interested in his work. Ed Young is a Chinese-American and our school was in Chinatown.

It was Wednesday afternoon when Mrs. Kotch came in and introduced Ed Young's books to us. We read **Lon Po Po**. We began to study about Ed Young, taking turns in a circle making comments about his books. We knew that he drew pictures with pastel colors. We made symbols to show the books he illustrated by using the letter I. The books he wrote and illustrated we left unmarked.

We wrote down many facts Ed Young said in his articles. We noticed that he drew and wrote differently than other writers and illustrators.

We began our Ed Young book search at the Chatham Square Library. We looked up and down, we walked back and forth, and our arms were loaded down with Ed Young books. We borrowed **Whale Song, High Up The Hill, Cricket Boy,** and many, many more.

When Mrs. Kotch came into our class she said, "I can't believe how many books by Ed Young you found. I didn't know there were so many." We set the books up every morning and we would pick out an Ed Young Book, read it and write about it.

We brought in articles and award speeches that Ed Young gave. We read them for homework and wrote new facts we learned.

We learned that his father's name is Q. L. Young. Ed Young has a wife named Filomena. He had 5 children in his family. His father built a house for Ed Young and his family to live in. When he was small, when it was time to eat Ed Young's mother would ring a bell and Ed Young would slide down the banister with his brothers and sisters. He was born in Teinsin, China and grew up in Shanghai. He came to America in 1951 to study and graduated

from Los Angelos Art Center. Mr. Young has illustrated more than 20 books for young people. Ed Young enjoys swimming and he practices T'ai Chi Chuan a system of exercise and postures practiced as self defense and meditation. We learned a lot about him from the speeches he gave and articles written about him.

When we were in the Chatham Square Library and the class showed such a great interest in Ed Young's work, the librarian told us that Ed Young had previously visited the library to talk about his books. Later, Mrs. Kotch asked Mrs. Grabler, "What would you like me to do on this project?" Mrs. Grabler said, "Get Ed Young!" They decided to try to contact his agent or if that didn't work the class would send an invitation directly to him. However, this all turned out to be unnecessary because of Ms. Ho.

One day in the teacher's room Mrs. Grabler and Ms. Ho had a conversation. The next day Mrs. Grabler told us about the coincidence. She also told us to speed up our project because Ms. Ho was going to meet Ed Young on the following Saturday.

When we were finished, the project included letters in English and Chinese signed by everybody in the class, a map of China, poems, and a crane inside a hexagon ball. Mrs. Grabler handed the invitation to Ms. Ho. Ms. Ho met Ed Young at his art exhibit in Tarrytown at MaryMount College.

When Ed young opened the invitation, his face lit up. He said, "Wow! This may be too good to resist!"

Later that week Mrs. Grabler received a letter from Ed Young. Everybody was clapping with joy because that meant he would be coming within the next 2 weeks. We later found out from Ms. Ho that December 10th was the big day. Ed Young was coming!

On Friday, Linda thought up a wonderful idea. Linda said, "Why don't we make a thousand paper cranes and give it to Ed Young when he comes?" But then

> November 16, 1992
>
> To Patrick Yiu man Kung Oscar Tina Lee 刘旭声 Tia Xing, 鍾国华 Daisy Seto Sydia Lam, Teresa, Brandon Linda Quanquan Xie, John Zhong yue yin Tam, Mike Zhong, Jenny Yu Melinda Ostig, Kitty, Amy Darrell Patrick, Mrs Grabler, Mrs Olvera Eric, Xu Sheng Lui, Darlene, mee Hong zhen
>
> Thank you for your praises and your invitation to visit your school in NYC. I shall be happy to come when I can make some time between all the things they-I must do before the end of the year.
>
> Your friend,
> Ed Young.

she suggested, "Why don't we make 999 cranes and let Ed Young make the last one?" Mrs. Grabler and the class liked Linda's idea. The people who knew how to make paper cranes taught other people in our class who didn't know. Mrs. Grabler gave us colored paper to make some paper cranes over the weekend.

On Monday, some people brought back a bunch of paper cranes. We put them in a box and added up all the paper cranes together. We had 365 paper cranes. We continued to make cranes in the afternoon.

On Tuesday, we finished folding the paper cranes. We had made over 1,200 paper cranes. We started to decorate the room, the main staircase, and the hallway. Mrs. Grabler suggested giving Ed Young the 1,000 paper cranes, but then she realized that there were 5 cartons of paper cranes, so she suggested hanging some of them from the ceiling of the room. Xu Sheng asked Ms. Olvera, the student teacher, if we could put the leftover cranes in the hallway and down the main staircase to the front door. We made a welcome sign for Ed Young to put on our classroom door. We wanted him to feel welcomed and comfortable.

On Wednesday, some boys decorated the door. Later that afternoon we finished stringing the paper cranes and hung them around the room. We finished putting up the signs and the paper cranes in the hallway and down the main staircase.

The big day had come when Mrs. Grabler came rushing into the room saying, "Ed Young is here!" Linda and Oscar went downstairs to escort him up.

Ed Young looked around the room which had cranes hung up and books that he had written and illustrated. It also had fact sheets about him.

Ed Young took out the book we sent him and read all of our names.

Mrs. Grabler asked Ed Young if he knew how to fold a crane. She told him about Linda coming up with the idea of making 999 cranes and letting him make the last one. He told us when he was coming back from Hiroshima, his friend George Letterson taught him how to fold the Chinese crane.

Linda got two pieces of paper and gave one to Ed Young. When Linda was teaching him how to fold the Japanese crane, Mrs. Grabler asked if we could ask him some questions. Ed Young said, "Yes" and we found out a lot of facts about him.

Ahem . . . Important Announcement! Before we go on we would like to say an old Japanese custom says that whoever has a thousand cranes can get one wish. Thank you, back to our story.

When it was almost time for him to leave, Mrs. Grabler asked if we could trade cranes. He said, "Yes" and it was time for him to leave.

Now that we told you the story, don't you wonder what Ed Young wished for?

These are Ed Young's Words!

"To get the story across for me, mostly it's the feeling. I think that if the book evokes a reaction of some sort, either positive or negative, I think it would have done what it is supposed to do."

"I don't have to listen to any discussion because feeling was touched— an experience was ignited and touched something real inside the person."

"For better or worse, as a foreigner brought up on Chinese legends and books, I was unaware of most classical children's literature and book awards in the West."

"What I didn't realize was that all the invisible threads of everyone and everything of the past, present, and future were being drawn together all the while."

"My guardian angel brought me to the U.S. and favored me with a scholarship to study architecture at the University of Illinois."

"My father was the Dean of Engineering at St. John's University in Shanghai and a senior partner in a construction company. He had hoped my artistic talent would develop along the lines of his trade."

"I have never lost the child in me. My father would spin endless tales of his own to entertain our imagination on summer nights lying on the flat roof of our house. I have never forgotten the images I saw in my mind."

After Ed Young left, we shared our feelings about the visit. Ming Zhi said that he felt great because Ed Young took the time to come to our school. Daisy also said it was a miracle when he came. Melinda and Amy said the same thing. I felt like screaming, it was so exciting. Kitty said, "Ed Young is so funny and had a good sense of humor. I hope to see him again." Darlene said that it felt like a dream. Then Patrick said, "When I saw him I still couldn't believe it." Jenny said it was a great experience. Linda also said it was an honor to escort him to our room.

We learned a lesson from all of this. We learned that nothing is impossible if you put your mind to it.

Our Learnings

We learned that being famous doesn't mean that someone has to be rich. By putting a lot of effort into our work, we made Ed Young happy and interested in meeting us. We learned that an American name is hard to transfer into a Chinese name. Ed Young was funny. When Darrell asked him his name in Chinese, Ed Young said Darrell. He also showed us how he flapped his ears better than the paper crane could flap its wings.

The End

Children's artwork and text:

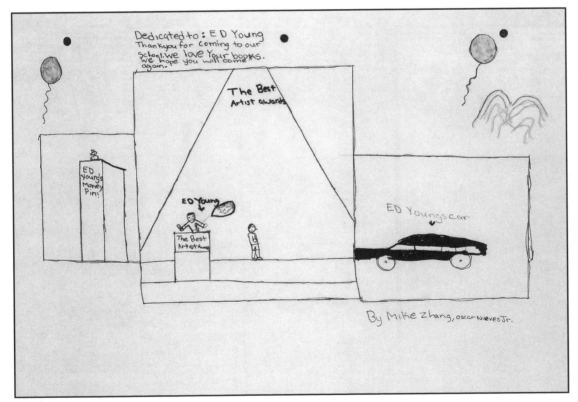

Dedicated to...

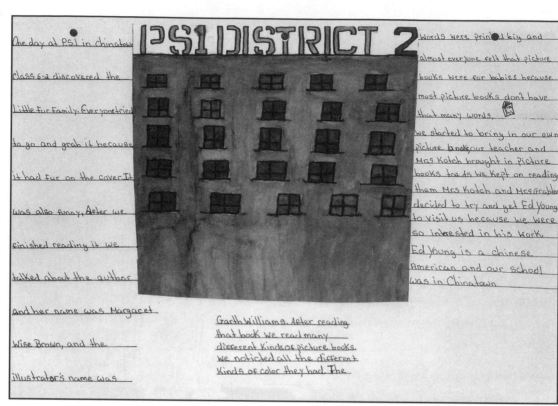

One day at PS1 in chinatown class 6-a discovered the Little Fur Family. Everyone tried to go and grab it because it had fur on the cover. It was also funny. After we finished reading it we talked about the author and her name was Margaret Wise Brown, and the illustrator's name was Garth Williams. After reading that book we read many different kinds of picture books. We noticed all the different kinds of color they had. The Words were printed big and almost everyone felt that picture books were for babies because most picture books don't have that many words. We started to bring in our own picture books our teacher and Mrs Kotch brought in picture books too. As we kept on reading them Mrs Kotch and Mrs Grabler decided to try and get Ed Young to visit us because we were so interested in his work. Ed Young is a chinese American and our school was in Chinatown

One day at P.S. 1...

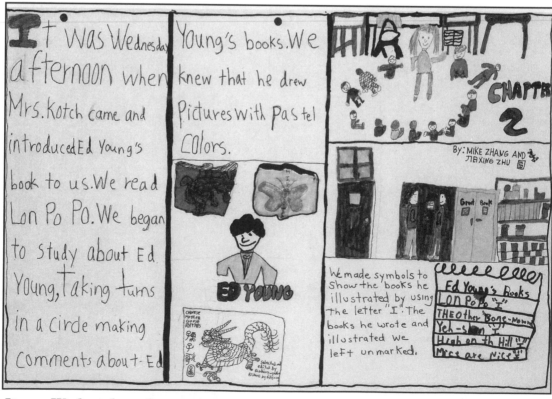

It was Wednesday afternoon when Mrs. Kotch came and introduced Ed Young's book to us. We read Lon Po Po. We began to study about Ed Young, Taking turns in a circle making comments about Ed Young's books. We knew that he drew pictures with pastel colors.

ED YOUNG

We made symbols to show the books he illustrated by using the letter "I". The books he wrote and illustrated we left unmarked.

Ed Young's Books
Lon Po Po "I"
THE Other Bone-Mouth
Yeh-shen "I"
High on th Hill "I"
Mrcs are Nice "I"

CHAPTER 2

BY: MIKE ZHANG AND JIAXING ZHU

It was Wednesday afternoon...

We wrote down...

We began our Ed Young book search...

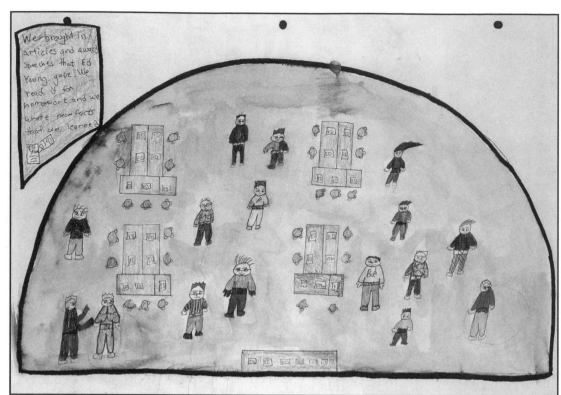

We brought in articles...

We learned...

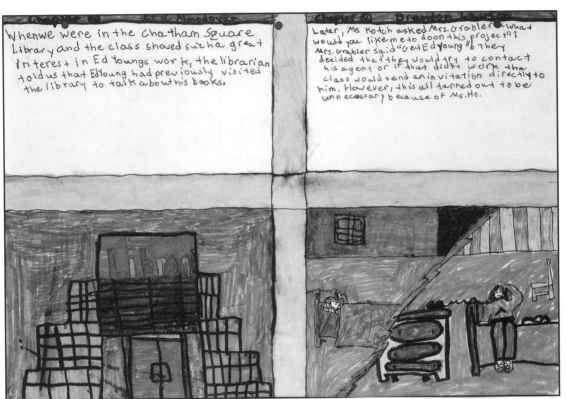

Whenwe were in the Chatham Square Library and the class shoved such a great interest in Ed Youngs work, the librarian told us that Ed Young had previously visited the library to talk about his books.

Later, Ms Kotch asked Mrs. Grabler "What would you like me to do on this project"? Mrs. Grabler said "Get Ed Young" They decided that they would try to contact his agent or if that didn't work the class would send an invitation directly to him. However, this all turned out to be unnecessary because of Ms. Ho.

When we were at the Chatham Square Library...

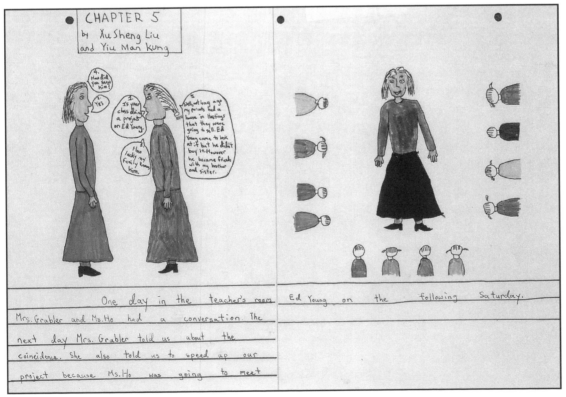

CHAPTER 5
by Xu Sheng Liu and Yiu Man Kung

One day in the teacher's room Mrs. Grabler and Ms. Ho had a conversation. The next day Mrs. Grabler told us about the coincidence. She also told us to speed up our project because Ms. Ho was going to meet Ed Young on the following Saturday.

One day in the teacher's room...

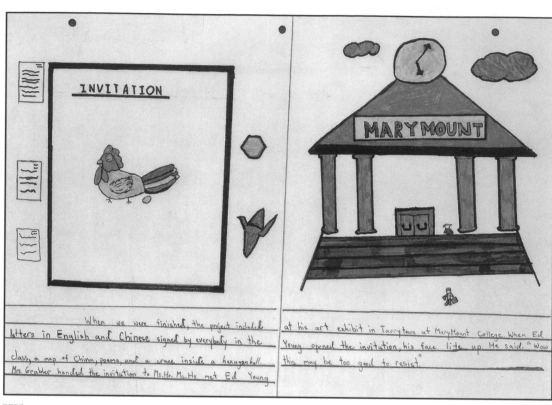

When we were finished, the project included letters in English and Chinese signed by everybody in the class, a map of China, poems, and a crane inside a hexagonball. Mrs. Grabler handed the invitation to Ms. Ho. Ms. Ho met Ed Young at his art exhibit in Tarrytown at MaryMount College. When Ed Young opened the invitation, his face lite up. He said. "Wow this may be too good to resist."

When we were finished...

CHAPTER 6 - by: DAISY SETO & OSCAR NIEVES

Later that week Mrs. Grabler received a letter from Ed Young.

Everybody was clapping with joy because that meant he would be coming within the next 2 weeks.

We later found out from Ms. Ho that December 10th was the big day. Ed Young was coming!

Later that week...

Chapter 7

Kitty Chan, Mei Hong Zhen, Yu Yin Tam

On Monday some people brought back a bunch of paper cranes. We put them in a box and added up all the paper cranes together. We had 365 paper cranes. We continued to make cranes in the afternoon.

On Friday, Linda thought up a wonderful idea. Linda said,"Why don't we make a thousand paper cranes and give it to Ed Young when he comes?" But then Linda suggested,"Why don't we make 999 cranes and let Ed Young make the last one?" Mrs. Grabler and the class liked Linda's idea. The people who knew how to make paper cranes taught other people in our class who didn't know. Mrs. Grabler gave us colored paper to make some paper cranes over the weekend.

On Friday...

On Wednesday some boys decorated the door. Later that afternoon, we finished stringing the paper cranes and hung them around the room. We finished putting up the signs and the paper cranes in the hallway and down the main staircase.

On Tuesday we finished folding the paper cranes. We had made over 1200 paper cranes. We started to decorate the room, the main staircase, and the hallway. Mrs Grabler suggested giving Ed Young the 1,000 paper cranes, but then she realized that there were five cartons of paper cranes. We knew Ed Young couldn't carry all those paper cranes, so Mrs.Grabler suggested hanging some of them from the ceiling in the room. Xu sheng asked Ms.Olvera if we could put the left over cranes in the hallway and down the main staircase to the front door. We had to make a welcome sign for Ed Young to put on our classroom door. We wanted him to feel welcomed and comfortable.

On Tuesday...

Ed Young is here!

Ed Young looked...

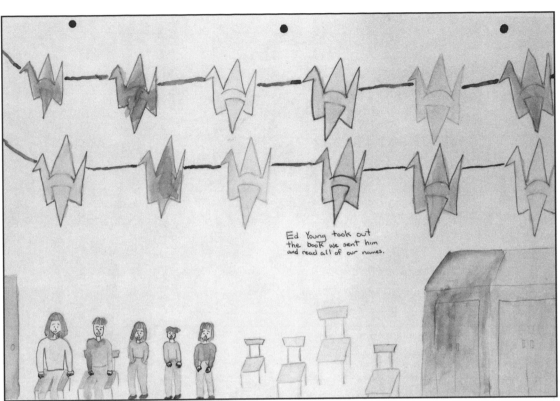

Ed Young took out the book...

Mrs. Grabler asked...

Linda got two pieces...

Ahem...

Now that we told...

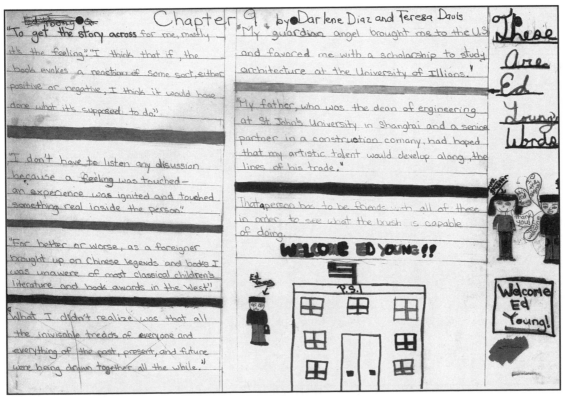

Chapter 9 by Darlene Diaz and Teresa Davis

"To get the story across for me, mostly it's the feeling." "I think that if, the book evokes a reaction of some sort, either positive or negative, I think it would have done what it's supposed to do."

"I don't have to listen any discussion because a feeling was touched—an experience was ignited and touched something real inside the person."

"For better or worse, as a foreigner brought up on Chinese legends and books I was unaware of most classical children's literature and book awards in the West!"

"What I didn't realize was that all the invisable treads of everyone and everything of the past, present, and future were being drawn together all the while."

"My guardian angel brought me to the U.S. and favored me with a scholarship to study architecture at the University of Illions."

"My father, who was the dean of engineering at St. John's University in Shanghai and a senior partner in a construction comany, had hoped that my artistic talent would develop along the lines of his trade."

That person has to be friends with all of these in order to see what the brush is capable of doing.

WELCOME ED YOUNG!!

P.S.

These Are Ed Young's Words

Welcome Ed Young!

These are Ed Young's words...

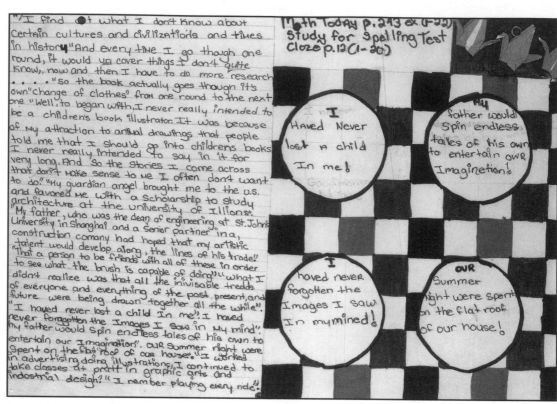

"I find out what I don't know about Certain cultures and civilizations and times in history "And every time I go though one round, it would up cover things I don't quite know, now and then I have to do more research . . . . . "So the book actually goes though it's own "change of clothes" from one round to the next one "Well, to began with, I never really intended to be a children's book illustrator. It was because of my attraction to animal drawings that people told me that I should go into childrens books I never really intended to say in it for very long. And so the stories I come across that don't make sense to me I often don't want to do." "My guardian angel brought me to the u.s. and favored me with a scholarship to study architecture at the university of Illions". "My father, who was the dean of engineering at St. John's University in Shanghai and a senior partner in a construction comany had hoped that my artistic talent would develop along the lines of his trade". "That a person to be friends with all of these in order to see what the brush is capable of doing" "what I didn't realize was that all the invisable treads of everyone and everything of the past, present, and future were being drawn together all the while". "I hayed never lost a child In me". "I haved never forgotten the Images I saw in My mind". "My father would spin endless tales of his own to entertain our imagination". "Our summer night were spent on the flat roof of our house". "I worked in advertising doing illustrations, I continued to take classes at pratt in graphic arts and indostrial design". "I rember playing every ride".

Math Today p. 293 ex (1-22) Study for Spelling Test Cloze p. 12 (1-20)

I
I Haved Never lost a child In me! Goodmorning Ed Yo

My
father would Spin endless tales of his own to entertain owr Imagination!

I
haved never forgotten the Images I saw In my mined!

OUR
Summer night were spent on the flat roof of our house!

My father was dean...

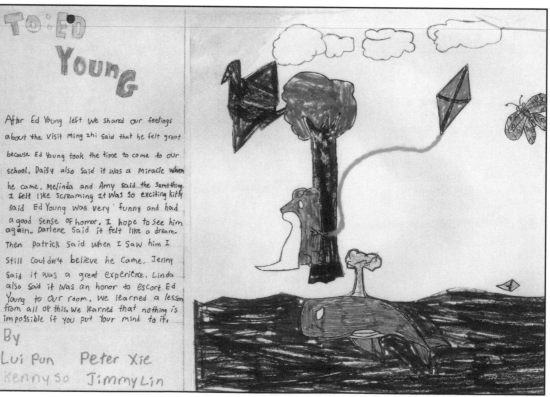

TO: ED YOUNG

After Ed Young left we shared our feelings about the visit Ming Zhi said that he felt great because Ed Young took the time to come to our school. Daisy also said it was a miracle when he came. Melinda and Amy said the something. I felt like screaming it was so exciting kiffy said Ed Young was very funny and had a good sense of homor. I hope to see him again. Darlene said it felt like a dream. Then patrick said when I saw him I still couldn't believe he came. Jenny said it was a great experience. Linda also said it was an honor to escort Ed Young to our room. We learned a lesson from all of this. We learned that nothing is impossible if you put your mind to it.

By
Lui Pun   Peter Xie
Kenny so   Jimmy Lin

To Ed Young...

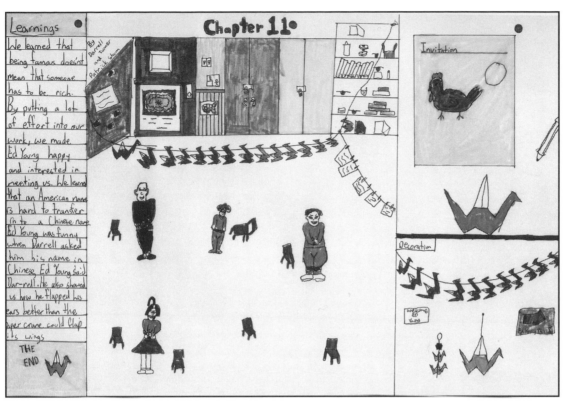

Chapter 11

Learnings

We learned that being famous doesn't mean that someone has to be rich. By putting a lot of effort into our work, we made Ed Young happy and interested in meeting us. We learned that an American name is hard to transfer in to a Chinese name. Ed Young was funny when Darrell asked him his name in Chinese. Ed Young said Darrell. He also showed us how he flapped his ears better than the paper crane could clap its wings.

THE END

Invitation

Decoration

WELCOME ED YOUNG

Our Learnings...

Chapter

8

A Sample Illustrator Study:
Peter Catalanotto

We've explored the many possibilities of studying authors with our classes, and now we'd like to highlight another key component of wonderful books— illustrations.

For many readers, it's the illustrations that draw them to books and hold their interest throughout. When a story is well told through an illustrated text, pictures and words work together to help the reader create and enhance meaning. Young emergent readers, as well as some fluent readers, focus their attention on illustrations before text, using pictures as their primary source of story. Likewise, young writers develop their own sense of story with their own pictures that truly are worth a thousand words. Students with a special interest in art may especially appreciate the illustrator's craft. It is for all of these reasons that we also study illustrators with our students.

> Our Noticings About Dylan's Day Out
>
> **About The Illustrations**
>
> • There are a lot of black and white things and animals.
>
> • Some things are in color.
>
> • He uses picture boxes.
>
> • There are lots of shadows.
>
> • He shows how things would look if you looked down at them.
>
> • Things happen in the pictures that aren't in the words.
>
> **About The Story**
>
> • Dylan got in trouble but he was a hero.
>
> • There aren't a lot of words.
>
> • It was funny.
>
> • He surprises you.

In earlier chapters we have presented some possibilities for looking at a body of an author's work. All hold true for an illustrator study, including:

➥ carefully selecting an illustrator whose artistic style is appealing and accessible to students;

➥ creating an inviting environment by gathering together books, biographical information, materials, and a place to experiment with the illustrator's style;

➥ making connections between students and the illustrator through activities and techniques that reveal the craft and style of the illustrator, such as art activities that explore artistic perception and point-of-view; and

➥ teaching and providing time to meaningfully practice the skills and strategies acquired through the study, for example using an illustration to extend the meaning of the text.

An illustrator study implies that the spotlight is on a body of artwork, which will give direction to the types of activities students engage in as they explore how pictures and text combine to create a total presentation of a story. You'll see how this unfolds in an author/illustrator study of Peter Catalanotto. What we will present here is a compilation of sessions that several classes have participated in. We chose Peter Catalanotto as the subject of our illustrator study because his paintings and text have broad appeal. As an author and illustrator, Peter knows how to adapt his presentations for students of various ages, revealing and sharing his craft with appropriate depths of understanding. For these reasons, we often study his work with students of all ages. Because of our relationship with Peter (which we'll tell you about in Chapter 11), we have been able to arrange for him to visit at schools where we work as staff developers, which does make for a wonderful way to celebrate a study. However, the activities stand on their own and don't require an "in-person" visit. We thought that sharing the components of this study through teachers' words would bring the experience closer to you and show the many possible directions a study can take.

Launching the Study

First-grade teacher: "I decided to begin our study with the first book Peter wrote and illustrated himself, *Dylan's Day Out*. I told students that I chose to share this book during one of our read-aloud sessions because I thought the illustrations were interesting. I asked them to pay special attention to the illustrations and be prepared to share what they noticed and thought after the readaloud. This chart summarizes their responses during our discussion."

Third-grade teacher: "I displayed Peter Catalanotto's books along the chalk rail in the front of the room during lunch one day. When my students returned from lunch, they immediately noticed the new books and asked

Things We Want To Ask Peter Catalanotto

- Why do you use so much black + white?
- Where did you learn to be such a great painter?
- How do you get your ideas?
- What's your favorite book?
- Do you like illustrating for other authors or writing your own?
- How do you paint from different perspectives?
- What's true in your books?
- Which illustrators do you admire?

the author's choice of topic, they may begin to think about topics they'd like to write about.

Other mini-lessons may focus on strategies the author uses to collect information, the choice of illustrations and genre, the use of language, techniques for sneaking in details, methods of grabbing reader's interest, and how the author chose to begin and end the text. Each mini-lesson can lead to whole-class, small-group, or individual investigations. Information students gather about an author's craft can become a blueprint to follow for their own content writing. Letters to the author are another technique for connecting learning and often begin ongoing communication with the author as mentor. Writing original nonfiction books is a wonderful culminating activity and helps assess and evaluate students' learnings.

My Side of the Mountain					by Jean George	
Kinds of Trees	Foods	Nuts + Berries	Animals	Birds	Flowers	Plants
Hemlock Tree Beech Tree Maple Trees Pine Trees Dogwood Trees Ash Trees Apple Trees Oak Trees	Acorn Pancakes Blueberry Jam fish Cattails + arrow leaf birds froglegs turtles rabbit strawberries	walnuts blueberries strawberries	weasel squirrel deer insects racoon insects beetles frogs turtles rabbits	woodpeckers chickadees falcon setter nuthatches whipporwhill duck hawk	dandelions yellow lillies Insects Crickets beetles cicadas	fern dandelions moss weeds

Chapter
10
Assessment and Evaluation

Assessment and evaluation are crucial to an understanding of literacy learning—they provide evidence of student growth, ongoing opportunities for conversations that document learning, and insights into the process of literacy acquisition. It is the gathering of this information and the construction of meaning around it that informs our teaching and heightens our understandings. Assessment and evaluation are at the heart of the teaching and learning process.

Students immersed in an author study are continually engaged in the process of assessing and evaluating, reflecting on both an author's body of work and their own literacy acquisition. During an author study, much of the class discussion revolves around sharing reading responses, comparing the author's use of techniques and writing strategies, and establishing criteria of excellence and standards for evaluation. At the same time, author studies provide teachers and students with numerous opportunities to collect evidence of student growth. This complete assessment documents learning, evaluates progress, and promotes opportunities to reflect on the reading and writing process. Thus, teachers and students are continually assessing and evaluating as an author study progresses.

As we know, not only are reading and writing two sides of the same coin, so too are assessment and evaluation. They are interrelated and cannot be separated. As you collect evidence of student literacy development in the daily context of an author study, you can also create standards of excellence, evaluate learning, and make short- and long-term teaching decisions. In order to clarify the issue, we've outlined some of our key beliefs about assessment and evaluation.

Assessment of student literacy occurs best while students are engaged in reading and writing. As students read, talk, and write about an author's body of work, opportunities to collect evidence of their literacy acquisition naturally occur. Teachers listen to student conversations, confer with individual students and groups, and collect samples of writing. In addition, class share meetings and mini-lessons provide opportunities to assess whole-class understandings and progress. This informal assessment allows teachers to interact with students around books, reader to reader, within the regularly scheduled reading-writing period.

Assessment is ongoing and occurs both as part of daily author study activities and over the duration of the author study. As students are engaged in an author study, their daily reading and writing responses document their literacy growth. Because this assessment is ongoing and occurs over the duration of the author study, there is a multitude of documentation for each student. Teachers and students then have the opportunity to cooperatively assess and evaluate this evidence. Individual students and groups share their reflections about their daily and cumulative learning with the class community.

⇸ Assessment is holistic and includes cognitive, social, and affective behaviors. Opportunities to observe students as they interact with their peers around author studies provide a focus on the whole student: his or her thinking, feelings, attitudes, and social interactions. Evidence collected from students' talking, listening, reading, and writing provides a complete picture of their growth in literacy, as well as their growing proficiency in relating effectively to peers, working cooperatively, and contributing to the class community.

⇸ Assessment informs short- and long-term teaching practice. As evidence is collected and analyzed by teacher and students, they are able to cooperatively plan mini-lessons, activities, and projects. Teachers are able to reflect on their daily teaching to determine what works best and why, as well as what doesn't work and how to make it more successful. Each completed author study enables teachers to assess and reflect on their long-term teaching practices and continually refine their strategies.

⇸ Criteria for excellence and evaluation are cooperatively established by students, teacher, and parents. As an author study progresses, students cooperatively determine criteria for excellence in responding to an author study; criteria for an A+ author study response log; or criteria for an A+ author study project. These expectations are clearly stated and guide the process of interacting with the author and culminating the study.

Students cooperatively examine and analyze the evidence of their learning. They evaluate their progress based on the established criteria and reflect on both content and process. Teachers also assume a reflective stance as they analyze individual student progress, class progress, and their own professional growth.

In addition, as they study an author's craft, students begin to establish criteria for excellence, such as Things My Author Does Well or What Makes My Author An Excellent Writer. These standards guide students' original writing efforts and help move the class toward established excellence.

⇸ Complete assessment involves collecting a wide variety of kinds of evidence of student growth. Evidence comes from daily author study activities and may include anecdotal records, lists, letters, webs, interviews, surveys, artwork, original writing samples, audiotapes, photographs, performances, and more. This evidence, along with student reflections about the process of learning, is the heart of assessment and serves to document student growth.

Over the years we've collected boxes and boxes full of student writing from author study notebooks and class charts. These samples have reassured us as to the value of author studies, reminded us of wonderful creative ideas, inspired new activities, and convinced us again and again of the powerful literacy learning acquired during author studies. We encourage you to begin collecting samples of your students' writing and urge you to take time to cooperatively reflect on the evidence with your students and colleagues.

Kinds of Evidence in Author Study Notebooks and Class Charts

LISTS
Books read during study
Noticings about authors
Wonderings and guesses about author
Ratings of books based on criteria
of excellence
Strategies author uses; strategies
reader/writer uses
What I Know About Author
Before Study/After Study

LETTERS
Reflective of process and content of study
Evaluative
To other readers
To parents
To teacher
To author

WEBS
Character study
Main idea and details
Author information
Setting
Events

VENN DIAGRAMS
Comparing characters
Comparing books
Comparing reader and character, reader and author
Comparing authors

RELATIONSHIP MAPS
Characters, authors

TIME LINES
Events in the book
Copywrite dates of books author has written

ATTRIBUTE CHARTS
Analysis of characteristics of individual book
Comparison of attributes of several books (illustrated below
and following pages)

Our Eric Carle Author Study		
Title	What does he teach us?	What does he do to make this book special?
The Secret Birthday Message	• shapes • how to follow directions • how to use a message	• there are cut out shapes • the pages are different sizes
The Very Hungry Caterpillar	• Days of the week • Caterpillars will change to butterflies	• There are holes on the pages • The pages are cut into diff. sizes

Title	What does he teach?	Special parts
Animals Animals	• many kinds of animals and insects • many poems	• a poem on every page • index of animals in the last pages • index of first lines
The Very Busy Spider	• how a spider web is formed • step by step instruction of spinning a web • can touch the thread	• how a spider spins a web • the web is raised up so we can do a rubbing.

Title	What does he teach?	Special Part
1, 2, 3 To The Zoo	• animal names • numbers • counting • colors	• train on the bottom of the page • the last page opens up
Pancakes, Pancakes!	• how to make pancakes • how to get the ingredients • Where do many things come from	• pictures of a mill • different tools

Title	What does he teach us?	Special parts
The Grouchy Lady bug	• Don't be so grouchy. • Try to be friendly.	• Shows each hour of the clock. • The words are getting bigger • The papers are cut, from the smallest to the biggest.
Polar Bear, Polar Bear, What Do You Hear?	• All kinds of animals and the sounds they make.	• Each animal is painted on two pages. • He uses many colors.

Title	What does he teach?	Special parts.
The Very Quiet Cricket	• about crickets • ways to greet each other • names of insects	• makes a musical cricket sound at the end
Draw Me a Star	• how to draw stars • how to follow directions	• there's a letter from Eric Carle in the back page • Step by step instruction for drawing a star

SURVEYS
Individual students' reading attitudes and behaviors
Class ratings of authors' books
Schoolwide ratings of books

INTERVIEWS
Characters
Authors
Students

ARTWORK
Illustrations of scenes
Innovations of texts
Posters

ORIGINAL WRITINGS
Innovations of texts
Prequels, sequels, changes in beginnings and endings
Plays
Big books
Songs
Poetry
Storyboards
Newspapers
Recipes
Commercials

PERFORMANCES AND CULMINATING ACTIVITIES
Dramatic readings
Music, dance
Radio shows

Not all evidence comes in written form. Often assessment in an author study begins with evidence you overhear. Kids might be talking on the lunch line about an author you are studying. A parent may comment about a child's urgency to visit the bookstore to buy another book by the author the class is studying. The class may let you know they love an author by applauding when the name of the author is mentioned or begging for extra time to study the author. The school librarian may inform you that books by the author you are studying are impossible to keep on the library shelf. During silent reading time books by the author you are studying are constantly being read and reread. You may notice students who never before asked to borrow books are now taking home books by the class author. In one classroom every gray-haired older man who walked into their room was suspected to be Eric Carle.

All these anecdotes are powerful evidence of students' growing connections with authors and books and their growing literacy acquisition. Many teachers keep a notebook in which they jot down anecdotes they overhear. You can organize these. Post-It™ notes are useful for recording anecdotes and are easily transferred to notebooks. Samples of teacher jottings follow:

1. During choice time every day this week m+s keep choosing to read + re-read the Eric Carle books.

2. Kids in yellow group asked to make their own version of Hungry Caterpillar.

3. P. (just beginning to speak English) ran to get 1,2,3, to the zoo to find the name of the animal he was illustrating for Class Big Book.

4. N.+S. volunteered to work together so they could share the Polar Bear, Polar Bear book and asked to recite the sounds for the class.

5. J. keeps touching the web in the Very Busy Spider and is determined to find out how to create his own web.

6. Noticed a few kids (R, B, S.) including indexes in their own writing.

Chapter
11
A Sample Schoolwide Model: Meet the Writers

Helping to create Meet the Writers at P.S. 321 in Brooklyn, New York, was one of the most exciting and meaningful experiences of our careers. Many of our colleagues knew the power of authors as mentors and had made contacts on their own with popular children's authors through letters or personal introductions, arranging for authors to visit with their classes. The excitement of these sporadic meetings inspired parents and staff members to join together to design a program that would bring authors to the school so that every student would benefit from this experience. Meet the Writers is in its fourth year and has become an institution at P.S. 321. This chapter describes how the program works and offers ideas for hosting author visits at your school.

Getting Started

Peter Heaney, principal of P.S. 321, along with Liz Phillips, the early-childhood coordinator, and other interested teachers were actively involved in brainstorming ideas to further the school's literacy initiative. At the end of the school year, Diane Grant, an active PTA member and a teacher herself, brought to the team her ideas for funding a program that would enable all students to make personal connections with authors and illustrators. We began the school year by drafting and sending a letter to all parents in the school community, accompanied by a brochure that outlined the program and invited participation. The brochure was distributed at local bookstores as well.

Dear Parents,

Over the past ten years at P.S. 321, staff and students have been building on a commitment to literature based reading and the writing process.

Both of these initiatives have led, on occasion, to classroom visits by writers and illustrators.

To further demonstrate our strong belief in the writing process and literature based reading programs, we want to formalize these author visits into a school wide program called "Meet The Writers."

We are looking to our school community of parents and friends for authors, illustrators, publishers, editors, journalists and printers to join in this exciting new program.

The accompanying brochure can be used to help you describe our program to people you know who would be interested in participating.

Please call Diane Grant at (718) 787-8543 for further information.

Sincerely,

Gretchen Hartman
P.T.A. Co-President

Adele Schroeter
P.T.A. Co-President

Peter P. Heaney, Jr.
Principal

MEET THE WRITERS

AT P.S. 321

1990–1991

At P.S. 321 in Park Slope, children learn to read through a literature based program. They also write frequently, learning early on to view themselves as young authors. With the literature based reading and writing process programs at the heart of our curriculum, staff members and parents have created a stimulating learning environment that strives to meet the needs of our diverse student population.

"Meet The Writers" is a project designed to bring our students in direct contact with members of the writing profession. When children meet with authors, illustrators, editors, journalists, publishers and printers, their understanding of the writing and reading process increases tremendously.

Enthusiastic young writers at P.S. 321 are interested in meeting with members of the writing community in intimate classroom settings. A 15 minute presentation, followed by a question and answer session, is extremely valuable to opening up the worlds of writing and reading. Please call Diane Grant at to learn more about how you can participate in this exciting program to enhance reading and writing connections for children.

Funding the Program

While we anxiously waited for some leads, Diane drafted a budget proposal and presented it to the PTA Finance Committee. Our professional development experience taught us the necessity of sometimes getting things going by starting small, so we planned on arranging for six author visits the first year—one for each grade (kindergarten through grade five). The PTA generously approved our request for $2,000 that we hoped would fund authors' honorariums, books to support related classroom author studies, film to take instant photos for autographing, and miscellaneous costs. This was so new to us that we weren't quite sure what miscellaneous costs we'd incur.

We knew that we wanted the visits to be special not only for our school, but for guest authors, too. As staff developers we knew the importance of setting the tone with food and flowers, and we appealed for support from local shops. We were thrilled when Cousin John's Bakery agreed to contribute dessert for our planned lunches with visiting authors on the day of their visit, and the Park Florist volunteered to provide beautiful bouquets of flowers to decorate our book displays, which the guest author could then take home.

In our search for funding sources, we did learn that grant money is available, some at the national or local level, through corporations, foundations, and local education grant programs. Many school districts now have professional grant writers to guide you through the process and pass on information about requests for proposals from foundations offering funding. We also learned that appealing to your parent body for help from someone with grant-writing experience may increase your chances for success. (For more ways to raise funds for a Meet the Writers program, see page 140.)

Making Author Contacts

Meet the Writers has been very successful in attracting many well-known children's authors and illustrators. It really all began with author/illustrator Peter Catalanotto. Many teachers, while reading and discussing Cynthia Rylant's work as part of an after-school study group, were particularly taken with the illustrations of *All I See*. The book jacket revealed that the illustrator, Peter Catalanotto, lived in Brooklyn! We told Diane, who then found his phone number in the directory and called him up to tell him about our new program. Peter told her that he had illustrated a few books for other authors and that he was awaiting the publication of a book he had written and illustrated himself.

Peter was interested in visiting the school but admitted that he had never presented and shared his craft with students before. Diane offered some advice: prepare slides that demonstrate your process; bring real artifacts such as book dummies, storyboards, or special tools; connect your talk to the authentic process that students go through in their own writing; and open up the session to questions at the end. Peter agreed on a date in December that would give us time to acquire his books and study his work in preparation for his visit (more about the management and preparation for an author's visit later on).

Discovering Peter Catalanotto on a book jacket was just one of the ways we've contacted authors. (It did inspire us to look up other names in the directory for authors and illustrators who lived in Brooklyn and this led to more dates for visits.) Sometimes we made contact through someone who knew someone. The wife of a teacher at our school knew Vera B. Williams and offered her an invitation that the author accepted. The local bookstore owner also arranged for us to talk to authors who lived in our neighborhood. One of the book distributors we used for ordering books for our literature-based reading program offered to help us contact an author. We've introduced ourselves to authors and illustrators we've met at conferences and invited them to participate in Meet the Writers, with some acceptances. And some authors who had visited and were so pleased with their reception and the preparation of the students referred colleagues to our program.

We were also delighted by the response to our brochure. We knew that our community included parents who were involved in the writing profession in some capacity, and we were overwhelmed by offers of visits from editors, typesetters, binders, authors, illustrators, photographers, and art directors. We knew that a school that used a process approach to reading and writing would benefit from meeting with varied members of the writing profession, and we began compiling a list of names to round out visits with children's book authors and illustrators.

We sent out letters of confirmation to our guests, outlining our discussion with them and listing the essentials of their visit. We asked what

Date

Dear _____,

We're so delighted that you will be visiting us to share your craft.

The date for your visit is _____. You will be meeting with readers + writers in the _____ grade. We've created a special meeting area for your presentation which will begin at _____ and end at_____

We invite you to join our staff for lunch and dessert following your presentation. Please take a moment to check off the materials that will be helpful to enhance your visit with us.

If you have any questions or requests, please call us at _____.

Sincerely,

Meet the Writers

Requests for Author Presentation

- ☐ Overhead projector
- ☐ Slide projector
- ☐ Drawing pad
- ☐ Markers
- ☐ Pencils
- ☐ Copies needed
- ☐ Travel directions
- ☐ Transportation
- ☐ Luncheon Menu Restriction

equipment they would need: slide projectors, screens, markers, large pads, etc. And we always invited our guests to join us at a luncheon with staff members on the day of their visit. Most were delighted to attend. Staff members who were available during the lunch period would bring their lunch and be treated to dessert and great conversation. Of course, the author was treated to lunch!

We were prepared to pay small honorariums to authors and illustrators because of our PTA budget and understood that some authors were too expensive for us. Some of our guests, in the spirit of community, offered to visit without a fee, and many who were just starting out were willing to join the program without payment because of the experience they were hoping to gain. Others understood the fiscal restraints of schools and requested very reasonable fees between $200 and $300. In any case, all guests benefitted from the experience and from the purchase of multiple copies of their books!

Preparing for the Visit

Once we completed arrangements with a guest, we had to decide which students at the school would be studying their work and meeting them. Our goal was to provide at least one visit per grade. We examined each author's or illustrator's books to help us assign appropriate grades. For instance, we knew that Vera B. Williams's work had wide appeal to students of many ages and that it was possible to study her work from several levels of understanding, but we ultimately decided that she would make an excellent second-grade visitor. Some authors made the decision for us by requesting a particular age level.

We scheduled far enough in advance to gather together books and other materials to support classroom author studies. We found that by ordering books through the publisher, we received a substantial discount for books for

author's appearance. For a picture-book author's visit, we usually ordered one copy of all the author's books for each class involved. In preparation for a novelist's visit, we would buy some titles in full-class sets, some in small-group sets, and some single copies for read alouds. The classes would share and rotate the books among themselves. Sometimes we were fortunate to have a collection already in place from our regular book orders for our reading program. The PTA budget helped fill out our collection.

The publishers were helpful in supplying us with promotional materials and biographical information. And we would search through our author files and regular sources of information to put together a packet for each teacher who would be involved in the preparation study.

Once the books and materials were in place, it was time for us to meet with the teachers in the chosen grade. Together we looked over books and other materials and began to discuss possibilities for classroom activities. We often agreed to meet again after everyone had a chance to read all of the books. These meetings provided all of us with wonderful ideas about how to use the books, and it was always interesting to see the different directions the classroom studies would take. Everyone usually included the activities outlined in Chapter 4 but also individualized the study to reflect the personality and needs of their class.

Planning for classroom activities was only one of the things we discussed at our meetings. Other topics we covered include:

BEHAVIOR EXPECTATIONS

We knew that active listening was essential, and so we reminded teachers to model and remind students about the body language and behavior of good listeners. Our students had high regard for members of the writing profession and had anointed them with movie star status. However, one of the main purposes of this program was for students to see the guests as mentors, and so we discussed the need to spend time in the classroom thinking about and formulating good questions that would yield inside information about the craft of writing and illustrating.

SCHEDULING

We worked out the scheduling of the actual visit. Because P.S. 321 is a rather large school with five to six classes in a grade, most of our guests agreed to present two sessions during a morning or afternoon visit so that two or three classes would participate in each session. Once in a while we did schedule a whole grade at one session at the request of the guest, but we pre

Author Jon Scieszka

ferred the smaller groupings. The sessions would be 30 to 45 minutes in length depending on the age level of the students.

As staff developers, we supported the classroom studies in several ways. In addition to meeting with the teachers as a grade, we often met with individual teachers to help them plan for their classroom study. This was a great opportunity to model some of the possibilities of author study activities with classes.

CREATING A MEETING PLACE

Another decision that had to be made was where would the visit take place? We wanted to create an intimate literary setting. We have used the auditorium stage with the curtains closed and children gathered on a huge old rug we purchased from a local carpet dealer. We have met in the school lobby in a similar fashion. Of course, the ideal setting is the school library, and this is where the Meet the Writers sessions are now held.

Here's how we create our intimate literary setting: We move the tables and chairs off to one side of the library. On the other side of the library is an armchair for our guest. Next to the chair, on a round table covered with a lace cloth, we display our guest's books and a vase filled with the donated flowers. It is quite simple yet elegant and adds to the special tone we want to create for this occasion.

OTHER DETAILS

Details that have to be arranged prior to the visiting date include arranging for flowers, ordering a cake for the staff luncheon meeting with the author, making a welcome poster for the guest to autograph, announcing the luncheon with a flier in staff mailboxes, sending out invitations to district and community members, and securing requested items for the guest's presentation.

MEET THE WRITERS

AT P.S. 321

Involving Parents

An author visit is a wonderful way to involve parents in their child's school experiences. Teachers let parents know about the classroom studies and often invite them to attend the visit. And parents love participating in and supporting fund-raising events (see page 140). Parents from the PTA volunteered time to help with the preparations and on the day of the visit. It seems to work best when a regular team of parents works with us to prepare and be there on the day of the visit, taking care of the many details, such as organizing the luncheon, that contribute to a smooth and pleasurable visit for everyone.

The Day of the Visit

From the moment a guest arrives at our school, we want to make every minute count towards creating a favorable impression. We like to be there in the school lobby to greet our guest and often arrange for a couple of students from the chosen grade to be there with us. This is when we show our guest the welcome poster and ask him or her to autograph it. We laminate these posters and proudly display them outside our library on our Meet the Writers Wall of Fame. It's exciting to watch the line of posters grow during the school year.

We ask guests to arrive about one-half hour before the first session and escort them to our meeting place. We use this time to help them set up any of their own materials and to take a number of instant photos to autograph. These author photos are given as a gift to each class (and help to discourage requests for autographs, which can be overwhelming).

Once students arrive, one of us introduces the author or illustrator and reminds students again about the role of good listeners. Copious notes taken during the sessions are typed up later and distributed to all staff members. We sometimes videotape the sessions with the guest's permission. We schedule about 10 minutes in between the sessions for the guest to relax and prepare for the next session.

We try to leave about 20 minutes in between the last session and lunch in order to spend time with the author and set up coffee, tea, and cake in the library near the display of books and flowers for the luncheon meeting. Teachers interact with the author and get further insight into the guest's craft. These insights become part of our notes to staff members.

At the end of the visit, holding an armful of flowers, leftover cake, a cer-

THINGS WE LEARNED FROM PETER CATALANOTTO

Write down all your ideas, for illustrations and words, when you brainstorm.

Circle the words you are not sure of spelling, and check them later on. Don't let the spelling stop you when you are writing down ideas.

Try using a story board to help you see the whole story at once.

Make pencil drawings and sketches before you illustrate with more permanent media.

Read your words out loud to hear how it sounds and help you decide if it sounds good to you.

Make a dummy copy to let you see how the book might look and help you figure things out. Then show it to someone to get suggestions about improving the book. (Peter's editor helped him understand he needs to put Dylan's feet in the picture)

The more you practice something, such as painting and writing, the more comfortable it becomes for you.

Write about things you care about and know about. (That's how Peter got the idea for Dylan's Day Out)

It's important to spend time on a project. (It takes Peter six months to work on a book)

Look at things around you in a new way for ideas. (Remember how Peter used his eraser?)

Mistakes can teach you new things. (Remember the paintings that dripped in Cecil's Story?)

Keep a journal so you can draw, write and collect new ideas and thoughts and things you never saw before. (Peter's old journal from college helped him get an idea for Mr. Mumble)

Don't throw any of your ideas away because you may want to use them some other time.

Here are some things Peter showed us about illustrating:
Leave a white spot on the eyeball to make them look shiny
Use your pencil eraser to help you shade and color
Show movement by blurring the lines
Use your finger to create soft shadows by rubbing it over pencil
Use photos to help you get ideas about what your drawing or painting could look like
Draw a third eye in the middle of a face to help you position real eyes and the nose

tificate of appreciation, and a powerful sense of an appreciative audience, our guest departs, usually eager to return.

Continued Support for Meet The Writers

Our initial budget of $2,000 from the PTA did get us through our first year of Meet the Writers. As we made more contacts, we realized that we could probably arrange for more than one visit per grade the following year, but this required additional money. In keeping with school tradition, we held a bake sale with great success and raised an additional $900! A winter holiday sale of books by authors who had visited and would visit in the future was held during an evening PTA meeting, yielding $500 more. We also knew that we wanted to provide an opportunity for parents who were not available during the day to attend a Meet the Writers visit so we planned a series of evening sessions for parents and children. Books were sold and our fund grew.

PS 321   MEET THE WRITERS

proudly invites you to a special evening with

MARILYN SINGER

author of
Turtle In July
Nine O'Clock Lullaby

Marilyn Singer will launch our annual schoolwide poetry festival by reading her poetry, sharing her creative process, and answering our questions. She will also give us a sneak preview of her soon to be published new poetry books!

Autographed editions of both hardcover books will be on sale. Looking forward to seeing you on...

April 27, 1992
PS 321 Auditorium
7:00 P.M.
childcare provided for young children
children in grades 3 and up are welcome to join us

Please turn this over for a Marilyn Singer Poetry Sampler ⇨

We are not working at P.S. 321 any longer, although we maintain strong ties with the staff there. When we bring visitors to the school, it is especially rewarding to see that the program is as strong as ever. Different staff members and parents have taken over the program responsibilities. The flowers and the cakes are still offered for the visiting days, the Wall of Fame is quite long now, and there are hundreds of delighted readers of all ages who have had the joy of experiencing a reader's dream of meeting the person who wrote the words or created the illustrations of the books they know so well.

Whether you are making arrangements for a single visit with an author or planning for an ongoing program, we hope our story will assist your own school community in preparing for a rewarding experience.

Appendices

Appendix A
Resources for Information About Authors and Illustrators
Books About Authors
Video Interviews
Audio Interviews
Author & Illustrator Birthday Calendar

Appendix B
Picture Book Authors and Illustrators

Appendix C
Author Study Survey

Appendix D
Checklist of Reading Behaviors

Appendix E
Teacher Response to Checklist

Appendix F
Invitation to Dialogue with Students

Appendix G
Parent Author Study Letter

Appendix H
Book in a Bag Parent Letter

Appendix I
Home-Reading Response Form

Appendix J
Family Reading Letter

APPENDIX A
Resources for Information About Authors and Illustrators

Books About Authors

Children's Authors and Illustrators: Corresponding with the Creators Of Children's Literature
edited by Barbara Allman and Marsha Elyn Jurca.
(Frank Schaffer Pub., 1991)

The Address Book of Children's Authors and Illustrators: Corresponding with The Creators Of Children's Literature
by Howard Blount.
(T. S. Denison & Co., Inc., 1994)

Books Change Lives: Quotes to Treasure
(The American Library Association, 1994)

Talking with Artists
edited by Pat Cummings.
(Bradbury Press, 1992)

Meet the Authors and Illustrators
by Deborah and James Preller.
(Scholastic, 1991)

Meet the Authors and Illustrators, Volume Two
by Deborah and James Preller.
(Scholastic, 1993)

An Author a Month (For Dimes)
by Sharon McElmeel.
(Libraries Unlimited, 1993)

An Author a Month (For Nickels)
by Sharon McElmeel.
(Libraries Unlimited, 1990)

An Author a Month (For Pennies)
by Sharon McElmeel.
(Libraries Unlimited, 1988)

Bookpeople (A First Album)
by Sharon McElmeel.
(Libraries Unlimited, 1992)

Bookpeople (A Multicultural Album)
by Sharon McElmeel.
(Libraries Unlimited, 1992)

Bookpeople (A Second Album)
by Sharon McElmeel.
(Libraries Unlimited, 1990)

Meet the Author Series
by Verna Aardema, Jean Fritz, Lee Bennett Hopkins, Rafe Martin, and Jane Yolen.
(Richard C. Owens Publishers, Inc.)

Once Upon a Time
by Reading Is Fundamental.
(G.P. Putnam's Sons, 1986)

Something About the Author
(Gale Research, 1971 – present)

Something About the Author Autobiography Series
(Gale Research, 1986 – present)

Meet the Authors (Volumes I – IV)
edited by Rozanne Williams.
(Creative Teaching Press, 1993)

Authors' Memoirs

A Grain of Wheat
by Clyde Bulla.
(1988, Godine, Boston)

A Girl from Yamhill
by Beverly Cleary.
(1988, Morrow & Co., NY)

Boy, Flying Solo
by Roald Dahl.
(1986, Puffin Books, NY)

Homesick: My Own Story
by Jean Fritz.
(1989, Dell Yearling, NY)

Childtimes:
A Three Generational Memoir
by Eloise Greenfield.
(1993, Harper Trophy, NY)

Little By Little
by Jean Little.
(1988, Viking, NY)

How I Came to Be a Writer
by Phyllis Reynolds Naylor.
(1987, Macmillan, NY)

Woodsong
by Gary Paulsen.
(1990, Macmillan, NY)

Bill Peet: An Autobiography
by Bill Peet.
(1994, Houghton Miffin, NY)

But I'll Be Back Again
by Cynthia Rylant.
(1993, Morrow, NY)

The Lost Garden
by Laurence Yep.
(1991 Julian Messner, NY)

Video Interviews

American School Publishers
Clarion/Houghton Mifflin
Harcourt Brace & Co.
Houghton Mifflin
Random House
Trumpet Club

Audio Interviews

Trumpet Club Authors On Tape
The Trumpet Club
P.O. Box 631
Homes, PA 19092-0631
(800) 826-0110

Scholastic Authors On Tape
Scholastic Book Clubs, Inc.
2931 E. McCarty Street
P.O. Box 1068
Jefferson City, MO 65102-6149
(800) 325-6149

On Becoming a Writer AuthorTalks
The Children's Book Council
568 Broadway
New York, NY 10012
(212) 966-1990

Information About Authors and Conferences

ORGANIZATIONS:

American Library Association
50 Huron Street
Chicago, IL 60611
(800) 545-2433

Children's Literature Association
Purdue University
210 Education Building
West Lafayette, IN 47907

International Reading Association
800 Barksdale Road
P.O. Box 8139
Newark, DE 19714-8139

PROFESSIONAL JOURNALS AND NEWSLETTERS:

Booklinks
American Library Association
50 East Huron Street
Chicago, IL 60611

The Horn Book Magazine
14 Beacon Street
Boston, MA 02108

Language Arts;
Primary Voices;
Voices from the Middle;
National Council of Teachers
of English
1111 Kenyon Road
Urbana, IL 61801

The New Advocate
P.O. Box 809
Needham Heights, MA 02194-0006

The Reading Teacher
International Reading Association
800 Barksdale Road
P.O. Box 8139
Newark, DE 19714-8139

The Five Owls
2004 Sheridan Avenue South
Minneapolis, MN 55405

Author and Illustrator Birthday Calendar

JANUARY

2   Jean Little
4   Phyllis Reynolds Naylor
14 Hugh Lofting
16 Robert Lipsyte
17 Robert Cormier
18 A. A. Milne
22 Brian Wildsmith
27 Lewis Carroll
28 Ann Jonas
    Vera B. Williams
28 Bill Peet
    Rosemary Wells
30 Lloyd Alexander
    Tony Johnston

FEBRUARY

1   Jerry Spinelli
2   Judith Viorst
3   Joan Lowery Nixon
4   Russell Hoban
5   David Weisner
7   Shonto Begay
8   Anne Rockwell
10 Stephen Gammell
    E. L. Konigsburg
11 Jane Yolen
12 Judy Blume
15 Norman Bridwell
20 Tana Hoban
25 Cynthia Voigt

MARCH

2   Leo Dillon
    Dr. Seuss
3   Patricia MacLachlan
5   Mem Vox
10 Jack Kent

11 Ezra Jack Keats
12 Virginia Hamilton
13 Diane Dillon
16 Sid Fleischman
20 Mitsumasa Anno
    Lois Lowry
    Bill Martin, Jr.
    Louis Sachar
21 Margaret Mahy

APRIL

2   Hans Christian Andersen
    Ruth Heller
8   Trina Schart Hyman
12 Beverly Cleary
    Gary Soto
13 Lee Bennett Hopkins
22 Paula Fox
25 Ann McGovern
    Alvin Schwartz
26 Patricia Reilly Giff
27 John Burningham

MAY

4   Don Wood
5   Marion Dane Bauer
    Leo Lionni
6   Bruce Coville
    Judy Delton
7   Nonny Hogrogian
9   Eleanor Estes
10 Bruce McMillan
11 Peter Sis
    Zilpha Keatley Snyder
13 Francine Pascal
15 Norma Fox Mazer
    Paul Zindel
17 Eloise Greenfield
    Gary Paulsen

18	Lillian Hoban
23	Margaret Wise Brown
	Scott O'Dell
25	Martha Alexander
29	Brock Cole

JUNE

1	Doris Buchanan Smith
2	Paul Galdone
	Helen Oxenbury
	Anita Lobel
5	Allan Ahlberg
	Richard Scarry
6	Peter Spier
7	Nikki Giovanni
10	Maurice Sendak
11	Robert Munsch
14	Bruce Degan
	Laurence Yep
18	Pat Hutchins
	Chris Van Allsburg
21	Robert Kraus
23	Theodore Taylor
24	Kathryn Lasky
25	Eric Carle
26	John Archambault
26	Charlotte Zolotow
30	David McPhail

JULY

2	Jean Craighead George
11	Patricia Polacco
	James Stevenson
	E. B. White
13	Marcia Brown
	Ashley Bryan
16	Arnold Adoff
	Richard Egielski
17	Karla Kuskin
23	Robert Quackenbush
26	Jan Berenstain
28	Natalie Babbit

	Beatrix Potter
31	Lynne Reid Banks
	Robert Kimmel Smith

AUGUST

1	Gail Gibbons
2	James Howe
3	Mary Calhoun
6	Barbara Cooney
7	Betsy Byars
9	Paricia C. McKissack
11	Joanna Cole
	Don Freeman
12	Ann M. Martin
	Walter Dean Myers
	Audrey Wood
16	Matt Christopher
	Beatrice de Regniers
18	Paula Danziger
21	X. J. Kennedy
28	Allen Say
30	Laurent de Brunhoff
	Donald Crews
31	Arthur Yorinks

SEPTEMBER

2	Bernard Most
3	Aliki Brandenerg
4	Syd Hoff
5	Paul Fleischman
7	Eric Hill
8	Byron Barton
	Jack Prelutsky
13	Roald Dahl
	Else Holmelund Minarik
	Mildred Taylor
14	John Steptoe
15	Tomie dePaola
	Robert McCloskey
16	H. A. Rey
21	Taro Yashima
27	Paul Goble

Bernard Waber
29   Stan Berenstain
30   Edith Kunhardt

OCTOBER

5   Gene Zion
6   Barthe DeClements
      Crockett Johnson
8   Faith Ringgold
9   Johanna Hurwitz
10   James Marshall
      Robert San Souci
11   Russell Freedman
14   Miriam Cohen
21   Janet Ahlberg
26   Steven Kellogg
27   Rachel Isadora
31   Katherine Paterson

NOVEMBER

1   Hilary Knight
3   Bette Bao Lord

9   Lois Ehlert
12   Marjorie Weinman Sharmat
14   Astrid Lindgren
      William Steig
15   Daniel Pinkwater
16   Jean Fritz
21   Elizabeth George Speare
23   Marc Simont
25   Marc Brown
27   Kevin Henkes
28   Ed Young
29   Madeline L'Engle
29   C. S. Lewis
30   Mark Twain

DECEMBER

1   Jan Brett
2   David Macaulay
19   Eve Bunting
22   Jerry Pinkney
27   Ted Rand
29   Molly Bang

APPENDIX B
Picture Book Authors and Illustrators

Verna Aardema (a)
Janet and Allen Ahlberg
Aliki
Frank Asch
Molly Bang
Byron Barton
Jan Brett
Marc Brown
Margaret Wise Brown (a)
Anthony Browne
Eve Bunting (a)
Eric Carle
Donald (i) and Carol (a) Carrick
Peter Catalanotto
Barbara Cooney
Donald Crews
Pat Cummings
Bruce Degan
Tomie dePaola
Leo and Diane Dillon (i)
Richard Egielski (i)
Tom Feelings (i)
Mem Fox (a)
Gail Gibbons
Ruth Heller
Kevin Henkes
Amy Hest (a)
Lillian Hoban
Nonny Hogrogian
Trina Schart Hyman
Thacher Hurd (i)
Rachel Isadora
Ann Jonas
William Joyce
Ezra Jack Keats
Steven Kellogg
Deborah Kogan Ray (i)

Robert Krauss
Leo Lionni
Anita Lobel
Arnold Lobel
Thomas Locker
Mercer Mayer
James Marshall
Robert McCloskey
Emily Arnold McNulty
David McPhail
Barry Moser (i)
Brian Pinkney
Jerry Pinkney (i)
Patricia Polacco
Ted Rand
Allen Say
Maurice Sendak
Blanche Sims (i)
Peter Sis
Lane Smith
Peter Spier
William Steig
John Steptoe
James Stevenson
Margot Tomes (i)
Chris Van Allsburg
Judith Viorst (a)
Bernard Waber
Rosemary Wells
Garth Williams (i)
Vera B. Williams
Don (i) and Audrey Wood
Arthur Yorinks (a)
Charlotte Zolotow

a = author only
i = illustrator only

APPENDIX C
Author Study Survey

1. Who are your favorite authors?

_____
_____
_____
_____

2. Why are they your favorites?

_____
_____
_____
_____

3. What connections do you have with these authors?

_____
_____
_____
_____

4. Are there authors you don't like? Why?

_____
_____
_____
_____

5. How do you discover new authors?

_____
_____
_____
_____

6. How can authors help you become a better reader?

_____
_____
_____
_____

7. How can authors help you become a better writer?

_____
_____
_____
_____

APPENDIX D
Checklist of Reading Behaviors (to be used with Appendix E on page 150)

I. BACKGROUND AND INTEREST IN READING

❑ actively listens when read to

❑ is willing to read

❑ enjoys talking about books

❑ vocabulary (listening, speaking, writing, reading)

❑ is persistent (sufficient attention span)

❑ selects books independently and appropriately

❑ is aware of and uses book language

❑ samples a variety of genres

❑ self-assesses as a reader

❑ shows confidence as a reader

II. ORAL READING BEHAVIORS

❑ stops reading when text doesn't make sense

❑ self-corrects

❑ uses a variety of decoding strategies

❑ structural analysis

❑ phonetic elements

❑ grammar (syntax)

❑ language (semantics)

❑ breaks words into parts

❑ blends parts into words

❑ recognizes sight words

❑ reads word by word

❑ emphasizes decoding

❑ maintains place in text

❑ notes errors which interfere with fluency

❑ reversals, repetitions, omissions, substitutions, insertions

❑ responds to punctuation

❑ reads with expression and fluency

III. ACTIVE INVOLVEMENT IN CONSTRUCTING MEANING

❑ expects text to make sense

❑ uses prior knowledge

❑ is willing to make guesses

❑ seeks confirmation in text

❑ uses illustrations (gross and finite detail)

❑ creates meaning from context and story structure

❑ understands complex sentence structure

❑ retells essence of the story

❑ skims and rereads to find information

❑ compares/contrasts elements of books and authors

❑ sets criteria for evaluation

❑ gets absorbed in text for sustained periods

APPENDIX E
Teacher Response to Checklist of Reading Behaviors

NAME _____

DATE _____

ASSESSMENT TOOLS:_____
_____
_____
_____
_____

COMMENTS ABOUT STRENGTHS: _____
_____
_____
_____
_____

COMMENTS ABOUT NEEDS: _____
_____
_____
_____
_____

TEACHING PLANS:_____
_____
_____
_____
_____

PARENT INPUT:_____
_____
_____
_____
_____
_____
_____
_____
_____

Date

Dear Readers,

For as long as I can remember, books have held an important place in my heart. I choose the books I read in many different ways. One strategy that I've been using all my reading life is to devour every book by an author I love.

When I was your age, my best friend introduced me to Maud Hart Lovelace and together we read all the *Betsy and Tracy* books. We spent hours talking about our favorite characters. That was my first shared author study.

This year we'll be studying authors together and writing to each other about our favorites, our wonderings, our connections, and our thoughts. A new author I discovered over the summer is Cynthia Rylant. I just finished reading *Missing May* and I love the way she uses beautiful language to describe life's simplest moments. She writes, "Before she died, I know my mother must have loved to comb my shiny hair and rub that Johnson's baby lotion up and down my arms and wrap me up and hold and hold me all night long." Even after I finished reading the book, it stayed with me and I wondered if Ob, Cletus, and the little girl would be all right without May.

I'd love to lend you the book so we can talk about it together. Write back and tell me about the authors in your life. Your letter will help me begin to know you as a reader and as a person. I can't wait to read it.

Sincerely,

APPENDIX G
Parent Author Study Letter

Date

Dear Parents,

Authors have always been important people in my life as a reader and perhaps in yours as well. Studying authors creates lifelong enthusiasm for reading and teaches important strategies.

Throughout the coming school year, your child will have the opportunity to explore many exciting authors. We'll choose them for a variety of reasons: to deepen curriculum understandings, to give insight into the writer's craft, and to broaden the reading and writing experiences of the students.

There are many ways for you to join and support our author studies.

➥ You are invited to visit our classroom and become a guest reader. Please let me know in advance so I can arrange for your visit.

➥ If you have author contacts or information, we'd love for you to share them with us.

➥ You can support our growing classroom library by donating books.

➥ Visits to the local library and bookstore with your child will help you conduct a home author study. Your child will be bringing home books to share with you, as well.

Please let me know if you have other ideas on how to become involved. We'll be launching our first author study on _____ beginning _____, and probably culminating around _____. We look forward to hearing about how you'd like to share authors with us this year.

Sincerely,

APPENDIX H
Book in a Bag Parent Letter

Date

Dear Parents,

Our literacy program is built on the belief that students grow into independent readers and writers when given chunks of time in school and at home to immerse themselves in meaningful print. Much of our day will be spent choosing and reading wonderful books and talking and writing about them.

My hope is that the excitement of learning together in school will enter your home when your child shares his or her reading with you. Each night your child will be bringing home in a bag a book he or she has chosen for home reading.

I invite you to become a partner in your child's reading life by devoting time to read each night. Here are some of the ways you can share books: reading books aloud to your child; listening to your child read aloud to you; taking turns reading aloud; talking about books; sharing your strategies as a reader, such as how you choose books for your own reading.

Our class has decided to use the attached form to help keep records of home reading. I thank you for your time, commitment, and willingness to become a reading partner with your child.

Sincerely,

APPENDIX I
Home-Reading Response Form

Name	Date	Title of Book	Parent Comments

Date

Dear Family,

We invite you to read this author's books together and write our class a letter about your reaction. You may want to share your wonderings, connections, noticings, or surprises. A class book of family letters will become a valuable contribution to our author study center.

Thank you for taking the time to write to us. We look forward to reading your words.

Sincerely,

Class _____

NOTES

NOTES

NOTES